Building better connections

Interagency work and the Connexions Service

Bob Coles, Liz Britton, Leslie Hicks

First published in Great Britain in November 2004 by

The Policy Press
Fourth Floor, Beacon House
Queen's Road
Bristol BS8 1QU
UK

Tel no +44 (0)117 331 4054
Fax no +44 (0)117 331 4093
E-mail tpp-info@bristol.ac.uk
www.policypress.org.uk

© University of York 2004

Published for the Joseph Rowntree Foundation by The Policy Press

ISBN 1 86134 661 1

British Library Cataloguing in Publication Data
A catalogue record for this report is available from the British Library

Library of Congress Cataloging-in-Publication Data
A catalog record for this report has been requested

Bob Coles is a Senior Lecturer in the Department of Social Policy and Social Work, University of York. **Liz Britton** is a Senior Policy and Research Manager at the Centre for Economic and Social *Inclusion*, London. **Dr Leslie Hicks** is a Research Fellow in the Social Work Research and Development Unit at the University of York.

The **Joseph Rowntree Foundation** has supported this project as part of its programme of research and innovative development projects, which it hopes will be of value to policy makers, practitioners and service users. The facts presented and views expressed in this report are, however, those of the authors and not necessarily those of the Foundation.

The statements and opinions contained within this publication are solely those of the authors and not of The University of Bristol or The Policy Press. The University of Bristol and The Policy Press disclaim responsibility for any injury to persons or property resulting from any material published in this publication.

The Policy Press works to counter discrimination on grounds of gender, race, disability, age and sexuality.

Cover design by Qube Design Associates, Bristol
Printed in Great Britain by Hobbs the Printers Ltd, Southampton

Contents

Acknowledgements

The research team wish to acknowledge with thanks the assistance of Claire Heathcote and Hanif Ismail in conducting and transcribing some of the interviews in the Northern Connexions Partnership and the help and cooperation it has received from all three Partnerships areas in which the research was conducted. We wish to thank the members of the three Partnership Boards, Local Management Committees and other stakeholders who generously gave their time and shared their knowledge and expertise with us. We also thank the young people, their Connexions Personal Advisers and other professional workers involved in trying to help and support them who have provided the case studies which lie at the heart of this report. Unfortunately they cannot be named here as we promised to preserve their anonymity.

We especially wish to thank the Chief Executives of the Connexions Partnerships and the Head of Strategy and Performance (Children's Services) from one of the research areas, all of whom also contributed to the development of the research and this report through membership of the Advisory Group. This met on several occasions during the course of the research and improved the content and structure of this report with their comments and suggestions. Other than the Chief Executives, the members were:

> Ian Chapman
> Paul Convery
> Alan France
> Divander Kaur El-Harti
> Viv McKee
> Tim Shiles
> Joyce Thacker

We wish to record our special thanks to Charlie Lloyd, Senior Research Manager at the Joseph Rowntree Foundation, for his good-humoured support and wise comments throughout the research process.

Building Connexions: the joining up of the elements of youth policy

The research on which this report is based was designed to examine interagency partnership working with young people. The encouragement of partnership working has been a hallmark of numerous initiatives developed since the 1997 General Election. Indeed, one report suggests that there have been more than 5,000 partnerships developed during the last six years (Skelcher et al, 2004). There is some confusion in the literature about the use of these terms so we should be clear about what we mean from the outset (Atkinson et al, 2002). We use the term *multiagency* to refer to situations where more than one organisation has dealings across a single issue and, perhaps, works with the same client. However, this does not necessarily imply that there is close or planned joint working. *Interagency* suggests that agencies *are working together*, that mechanisms through which different roles are assigned, and that joint-working practices are agreed. The main aim of the research was to examine how, and in what ways, such interagency work was being designed and delivered both in theory and in practice.

This research chose one major initiative within the development of policies for children and young people – the development of the Connexions Strategy – to examine issues involved in interagency work in some detail. Although the main research questions were formulated in 2001 – around the time at which Connexions Partnerships were being piloted across England – many of the issues examined in this report have continued policy relevance. Such issues lie at the heart of reconfiguration of services for children and young people, in the wake of the Green Paper *Every child matters* (DfES, 2004a), and the *Children's Bill* which is before Parliament as this report goes to press.

This chapter outlines the background to the research, the development of the Connexions Strategy, and some of the different ways in which Connexions Partnerships have sought to develop that strategy. The research deliberately set out to examine different approaches to partnership development and these are briefly described towards the end of this chapter (pages 6-9) and in more detail in the Appendix. Chapters 2 and 3 examine facets of interagency work in more detail, with Chapter 2 being based around detailed case studies of young people that examine the interface of multiagency work with daily lives. Building on these and other case studies, Chapter 3 analytically examines interagency work around issues concerning: referral; assessment of need; roles; responsibilities and protocols of joint working; brokerage of services and advocacy on behalf of young people; information sharing; and the management of partnership working across agencies. Finally, Chapter 4 returns to the implications of the research for the current policy agenda, including the development of Children's Trusts and subregional and local authority services and/or support for young people.

Policy background to the research

Announcing Connexions at London's Centrepoint on 16 December 1999, the Prime Minister, Tony Blair, made it clear that the Connexions Strategy was "our front line policy for young people" (DfEE, 2000, p 4). Since the first pilots in 2001, Connexions Services have been gradually rolled out nationally in three main waves so that, since 2003, they cover all areas across England. Forward planning now contains a vision for the strategy, taking it up to 2006 (Connexions, 2002g). This latter planning document repeats the ambitious aim for Connexions to bring together existing agencies such as "health services, police and probation, youth services, social services, youth offending teams, drug action teams, voluntary and community organisations, careers companies and many more ... to deliver a seamless support to all 13-19 year olds across all agencies". From the outset the strategy was intended to provide the means through which greater coherence could be developed within services for young people nationally, subregionally and locally, an ambition emphasised by the fact that the first strategy document was introduced by the PM and signed by no fewer that seven cabinet ministers. *A vision to 2006* is also produced under eight, albeit more junior, ministerial signatures (DfES, 2002). A recent review by the National Audit Office (NAO) suggests that this degree of authority has provided a clear mandate to local partnerships to seek and demand cooperation across agencies and departments (NAO, 2004). Clearly multi- or interagency and cross-departmental collaboration is thus central to the Connexions Strategy and is the focus of the research.

The Connexions Strategy and Connexions Service

At the heart of the Connexions Strategy is the development of the Connexions Service described in the initial prospectus for Connexions as, "a modern, public service that works in a completely different way", forging a new enterprise from across different services and agencies (DfEE, 2000). The intention has always been that the service would provide support to all young people through an allocated Personal Adviser (PA) who would "provide a wide range of support to meet the young person's needs and help them reach their full potential". The help provided is planned to include "information, group work, advice, guidance, in-depth support and access to personal and social development" (Connexions, 2002g).

Not in education, employment or training (NEET)

Despite being a universal service for all teenagers, the origins of the Connexions Strategy and service lie in a concern with the most

vulnerable young people, especially those most likely to become disengaged from learning, training or employment. Two left of centre think-tank reports had helped highlight attention to those young people who left school at minimum school leaving age but did not engage in post-16 education, employment or training (Pierce and Hillman, 1998; Bentley and Gurumurthy, 1999). Such young people, initially identified by academic researchers under the label 'status zero' (Williamson, 1997), later became more widely known in government publications by the term 'NEET' (not in education, employment or training). The two think-tank reports were closely followed by an official inquiry by the government's own Social Exclusion Unit (SEU) in their fifth report *Bridging the gap*. This 1999 report lamented the fact that an estimated 161,000 young people aged 16-18 (9% of the age group) were disengaged and, in line with the previously published White Paper *Learning to succeed*, announced a crucial attempt to remedy the situation, through a "single new advice and support service, in charge of trying to steer young people aged 13 and 19 through the system" (SEU, 1999). The report also emphasised that, although this was intended to be a universal service for all those in the age group, it was also to be targeted at those most in need.

The report outlined various known routes into disengagement and the over-representation of some groups of young people including: those with special educational needs or disabilities; young offenders; care leavers; young carers; and young women who become pregnant or parents. Disengagement at the age of 16 was also shown to be associated with earlier forms of disaffection and disadvantage: underachievement, truancy and exclusion from school, the subject of earlier SEU reports (SEU, 1998). Later research has attempted to put a financial cost on the disengagement of 16- to 18-year-olds (Coles et al, 2002; Godfrey et al, 2002), confirmed by the NAO as over £1.4 billion in the long term. The NAO estimate that the NEET group numbered around 181,000 in 2002, but that reducing this number by even 1% "would result in 1,700 young people re-engaging in education, employment or training with economic savings of £165 million" (NAO, 2004). One of the main targets of the Connexions Strategy, therefore, is a reduction in the number of young people categorised as NEET in 2002 by 10% by November 2004, and the NAO reports that many Partnerships are well on their way to achieving this.

Personal Advisers and their location

From the outset there was an obvious tension between the skills, training, resources and organisational requirements of a universal service and the more specialist support designed for the disengaged or 'hard-to-reach'. Some services pioneered by Connexions are provided centrally through Connexions Direct, a help and advice service accessed by telephone, text-messaging, e-mail or an Internet website. Other services are, however, dependent on face-to-face contact between staff (mainly Connexions PAs and young people). PAs may be located or based in a variety of different settings: One-Stop-Shops or access points on the high street; schools or colleges; community-based provision; and various forms of outreach facilities, including mobile provision designed especially for use in rural areas.

Although the budget for the Connexions Service is considerable at £450 million per year, even with nearly 8,000 successfully recruited PAs, difficult decisions have to be made about where they will be located, with whom they will predominantly work, what sort of caseload they will have and, because of this, the level of support that can be offered. The NAO reported that, if Connexions PAs were working with the caseload deemed manageable at the pilot stage, in excess of 15,000 PAs would be required. With less than 8,000 recruited, difficult choices have had to be made, and there is some evidence from the surveys conducted by the NAO and elsewhere that mainstream schools feel it is their resource that has been squeezed at the expense of efforts directed at trying to reduce the NEET group (NAO, 2004; OECD, 2003). Partnerships are thus, potentially, at times the origins of conflicts of interests as well as consensual collaboration.

Universal and targeted service

As both a universal and targeted service, many of the planning documents for Connexions made clear that different young people will need different types of support, and that services should be designed accordingly. Partnerships are

asked to identify the size and composition of three different groups of young people with different 'tiers of need'. Around 60% of young people are thought likely to require only general advice and support and minimal help in seeking information and advice in reaching career decisions. At the apex of the tiers of need are around 30% of young people who are anticipated as needing in-depth support to reduce the risk of not participating in education and training effectively, and up to a further 10% who may require specialist support in facing substantial and multiple problems. Given the interest of this research it is these top two tiers of need on which this project has focused attention as, for them, PAs are more likely to have to 'broker' in specialist services from a number of different professions to help them overcome their barriers to learning or training in a coordinated way (Connexions, 2001a).

The different organisational layers within Connexions

Prior to December 2003, the Connexions Service had a National Unit (CSNU) responsible for the coordination nationally of the service and located within the Department for Education and Skills (DfES). At the end of 2003, CSNU was replaced by the Supporting Children and Young People Group (SCYPG), although this had a much wider remit covering Youth Service programmes, volunteering programmes, aspects of the work of the Teenage Pregnancy Unit (formally part of the Department of Health) and the Children's Fund (formally part of the Children and Young People's Unit). The delivery of the Connexions Service is organised subregionally by 47 Partnership Boards across England. The Boards are drawn from a number of different agencies "which also include representation other key players including Local Education Authorities [LEAs], schools, colleges, the Learning and Skills Council (LSC) and Jobcentre Plus" (Connexions, 2002g). The Partnership is also often supported by a Chief Executive Officer of the Partnership and a senior management team. Some subregions are large and span up to 10 different local authorities, with local managers responsible for Connexions development within each local authority.

To aid the organisation of Connexions within each local authority, there are also Local Management Committees (LMCs) in each local authority, each drawing its membership from a range of agencies across the authority. Representation on the LMC invariably includes senior managers from the Youth Service, YOTs, health services (such as primary care trusts), the LEA, schools, colleges, the careers company delivering careers education and guidance, and the voluntary sector. Many local authorities have also developed a number of ad hoc committees concerned with day-to-day implementation issues, and designed to share and disseminate good practice. The organisation and management of front-line workers (the PAs) depends on which model of partnership development has been adopted by the Partnership Board.

Models of partnership development

In describing different models of Connexions Partnership development, the NAO concentrates on only two forms. The predominant of these is the so-called 'subcontracting' model with the Partnership based within a newly formed company, limited by guarantee. The Partnership then subcontracts with a number of different providers of front-line services, including careers companies, but also including at least 10% of business delivered through contracts with the voluntary sector. Other contract holders often include the LEA, the Youth Service, and other multiagency local partnerships such as YOTs or Drug Action Teams. It is also not unusual in the larger partnerships for one careers company to have contracts for the delivery of services across more than one local authority (or LMC area), or indeed for a careers company to hold contracts with more than one Partnership. All Partnerships also offer funds through other grant-making capabilities for 'capacity building' or 'service development' (particularly in the voluntary sector). Under the subcontracting model, a Partnership may have a complex array of contracts with a large number of service providers. This has implications for the VAT cost of such arrangements because of the large number of contracts, although it does allow for many organisations and agencies to regard themselves as a genuine stakeholder within the Partnership (see below).

The second major model of partnership development is variously described as the 'direct delivery' or 'transmuted' model. Here the Partnership is primarily based around an already established careers company, or a merger of companies, to which the extra functions necessary to fulfil the broader remit of Connexions are added. The recent NAO review suggests that, perhaps because the organisational structure of this model is more compact, these Partnerships have been quicker to deliver on issues such as the extent to which diploma training has been completed by its PAs (NAO, 2004). Partnership types, therefore, are likely to bring their own distinctive advantages.

The third model, outlined in the first OfSTED report on Connexions (but not covered by the NAO) is perhaps best seen as a variant of the subcontracted model. In this third model, however, the newly formed Partnership is not itself the legal and accountable entity. Rather this function is played by another 'lead body', such as a single local authority (OfSTED, 2002). Contracts and financial matters are thus handled by the lead body, rather than through the Partnership itself. In some instances, the lead body is also the main employer, including the employer of Connexions PAs other than those employed by a careers company. So, regardless of which setting the PA may be working in, (s)he is a local authority-employed PA. As well as being potentially attractive to PAs themselves, lead body Partnerships are able to draw on established management structures (including financial management expertise). Initially this model was not encouraged by the CSNU. Early in 2004, however, Partnerships have had to seek means of reducing their VAT liabilities or save money elsewhere. The lead body model has thus become a more attractive proposition, if only because it provides one way through which the number of contracts, and the consequent VAT bill, can be reduced (A. Weinstock, letter to Connexions Partnership chief executives, 2004).

Interagency and multiagency working

There has been a growing literature on multi- and interagency working, some of which is finding its way into the training material for Connexions PAs (Connexions, 2004). The literature distinguishes between different types of multiagency work. Atkinson et al (2002), for instance, describe five different models of multiagency working arranged along a continuum from "decision-making groups, where professionals from different agencies maintained their distinct role" through to "operational teams, where professionals worked in close proximity and therefore merging roles was more likely" (Atkinson et al, 2002). This suggests that another issue adjacent to the distinction between inter- and multiagency partnerships is the notion of multidisciplinary teams. Many would see such teams as desirable, and many Connexions Partnerships have aimed to build them. They do, however, present challenges associated with differences in professional cultures, practices and the training that develops and sustains these. In their research on *Multi-agency working,* Atkinson and colleagues do indeed further distinguish between different types of delivery models, and the ways in which these are supported by coordinated and multiagency consultation and/or training. As we will see, the various layers and levels of organisation and working within Connexions involve a range of different forms of multi- or interagency work, from needs assessment and service auditing, strategic decision making, planning implementation at a local level, through to service delivery. Given this, it is clearly important to distinguish between the issues being faced by different levels of the organisation that are charged with different tasks.

A key aspect in the design and delivery of Connexions Services is the deployment of front-line PAs. Although, as we will see below, the development of Connexions Partnerships has taken a different form in different parts of the country, in addition to their own specialist training (in careers education and guidance or youth work, for instance), professional workers taking on the role of PAs are required to undertake a nationally designed, diploma course training. The training material for Connexions PAs devotes one of its five modules to 'Working with other agencies and the community'. The CSNU has also jointly produced a number of booklets on *Working together,* outlining the requirements and options surrounding joint working with a number of partner agencies including, for instance, youth justice services, teenage pregnancy workers, the statutory Youth Service, voluntary and community organisations, youth homelessness agencies, and social services departments including work with care leavers and asylum seekers (Connexions, 2002a-f,

2003a). These are based on a number overarching principles concerning: the identification of the most appropriate worker to act as PA; information sharing between workers; ensuring consistency, continuity, accountability and quality assurance; and rationalising contact and avoiding duplication of effort. Both the PA diploma course and the more generally available 'Understanding Connexions' module also draws specific attention to some of the major barriers to effective partnership, including miscommunication, poor coordination, cultural differences in the working practices between different agencies, a lack of equality and respect between agencies, or a history of conflict or misunderstanding. Clearly, although partnership and interagency working sound like common sense, in practice they may take a huge amount of concerted effort to achieve.

The design of the research

There have been numerous research projects about Connexions despite the service and strategy still being in the early stages of development. Much of the research, however, has relied on quantitative methods only – in particular, extensive surveys. These have, necessarily, relied on simple questions administered by questionnaire or telephone interview to large numbers of people. Surveys have been conducted on both 'stakeholders' – some of the main partners on Partnership Boards and on LMCs – and on 'customers' – young people – the recipients of Connexions Services (DfES, 2004).

The research reported here has employed intensive qualitative methods. The project included around 300 hours of semi-structured, audio taped interviews, conducted over a period of two years. The interviews were 'semi-structured' so that the researchers could explore issues in depth. Through these we sought the views of 'stakeholders' within the Partnership Boards and LMCs, as well as exploring the views of young people about the various forms of professional intervention in their lives and those of the workers concerned. In order to explore the various layers of multi- and interagency work we examined three different levels of working:

• within the Partnership Board;
• within LMCs and managers of local agencies;

- front-line work: this was done through a series of case studies of individual young people, both from the perspective of the young person and that of the various professionals with whom they have been involved, including their Connexions PAs.

We tried to examine the relationship between these three levels to focus on both *policy intent* (as derived from documentary sources such as business plans and by key stakeholders) and *routine and actual practices* (as described to us by PAs, other professional partners, and by the young people with whom they were working). The case studies were broadly the same in all three areas in order to allow the research to examine how Connexions and associated partners worked with young people in similar situations. They included:

- a young person in Years 9 or 10 who is thought to be at risk of (or is) excluded (or self-excluding) from school;
- a young person (Year 12) with a statement of special educational need;
- a young person (Year 11 or older) 'looked-after';
- a young person involved in the youth justice system;
- a young person who is not living in the parental home;
- a young woman who is either pregnant or already a mother;
- a young asylum seeker;
- a young person disengaged from education, employment and training at age 16 or 17 (different subgroups were also covered for this category);
- someone disengaged from education, employment and training at age 16 or 17 but recruited from a voluntary sector or community-based agency.

In practice, many of these categories overlapped. Many of them also fell into the main Connexions priority group, either being NEET, at risk of being NEET, or having been NEET in the past. The case studies thus allowed us to examine how Connexions was working with its key priority group in partnership with other professional workers. Detailed illustrative descriptions of three of the case studies can be found in Chapter 2. It is, however, also important to the design of the research that the case studies were examined within specific 'contexts'. To do this the design of

the research took a vertical slice through the Connexions Partnership, from strategy and planning through to service delivery.

Because this research adopted an 'intensive' design, it could not be an extensive study of a large number of Partnerships. Instead the research concentrated on only three, and within two of these, on only one LMC area. The three Partnerships were chosen to reflect the three different models of partnership development: subcontracting, direct delivery and lead body. They were also selected for the reason of being socio-geographically varied with the three covering part of a large, multiethnic, metropolitan area, multiethnic cities and towns, and two of the three also covering extensive rural areas. The Partnerships were also at different stages of development, having commenced operations at different phases of the national roll out. A brief summary of the areas is given below and further detail can be found in the Appendix. The descriptions are based on around 90 hours of taped and transcribed interviews and the study of volumes of planning documents produced by the Partnerships.

The three research areas

The names of the three Partnership areas, and those of all those interviewed during the course of the research, are referred to by pseudonyms only. The first, Midland Connexions, was one of the early pilots and started operating in spring 2001. The second, Metro Connexions, had piloted some aspects of Connexions in separate boroughs in 2001-02, but did not start as a fully-fledged Partnership until the summer of 2002. The third, Northern Connexions, started in October 2002. Although Metro Connexions and Northern covered a large number of different local authority areas, we examined the planning and implementation of services in only one of these. In Metro Connexions we refer to the borough covered as Metborough, and the Metropolitan District in Northern we identify as Nortown.

Midland Connexions

Midland Connexions was the smallest of the three Partnership areas, covering just over 81,000 young people aged 13-19 from just two local authority areas. The area covered by the Partnership included one medium-sized city and a shire county, with a number of small- to medium-sized market towns. Midland Connexions Partnership was part of an economic and regeneration company, limited by guarantee, which directly employed most of the staff working for Connexions.

At strategic level, Midland Connexions Partnership Board was large compared with the others. At the outset, it was thought important for the Board to be as inclusive as possible in order to reassure potential partners of the importance of their role within the Partnership. Because the Board covered only two local authorities, originally there was a matching representation from each. When the Partnership became more established, the frequency of meetings was reduced and was described as having turned into a consultative forum supporting a more active Executive Group. The two LMCs of city and shire county were originally part of the organisational structure. These were not as large as the Partnership Board, and the frequency of meetings was also reduced over time. Liaison with the local authorities was carried out through informal meetings held around every two months between the Chief Executive Officer of Connexions, the local authority Chief Executive Officers, and the chief officers or deputy from education and social services.

As a direct deliverer of services, approximately 78% of resources were committed to service delivery itself. Many, but by no means all, of the 316 staff were previously employed by two careers companies (which ceased trading in April 2002) covering the two local authorities. Services were based on those provided to 'clients who are in education' or those who are 'out of education'. Specialist staff did outreach work to specific groups, for example, drug users, young offenders and so on. Other staff were located within partner agencies, such as the voluntary sector and YOTs. There was a policy of siting both Connexions and partner agency staff in the same locations. There were 35 Connexions sites across the region, including three One-Stop-Shops and, in total, around 165 PAs. One form of specialist provision was from a Learning Gateway Project, based at the Local Learning and Skills Council (LLSC). This had eight PAs, six of whom were based with life skills providers. This continued

after the Learning Gateway was replaced by Entry to Employment (E2E) in the summer of 2003.

Senior managers of Midland Connexions Partnership told us that they had long recognised that building an effective team was not something that was achieved overnight. It needed concerted effort at a number of different levels within the organisation and on a number of different fronts. They were also clear about the importance of political negotiation during the early stages of the development of the Partnership. They aimed to ensure that key stakeholders did not feel threatened by developments, but rather to recognise the advantages to be gained through cooperation; and managers were convinced that the effort involved was worthwhile. Most of this was achieved in individually tailored meetings rather than through discussion or debate within boardrooms. As well as this *horizontal* level of partnership formation, senior managers were also concerned that they had a responsibility to work *vertically* within the organisation and to communicate the company vision. Senior managers addressed this on a number of fronts: selling the vision; investment in training; rewarding innovation and progress; and building self-belief, pride and morale.

Metro Connexions and Metborough

Metro Connexions covered a number of boroughs across a very large city containing over 100,000 young people aged 13-19. The boroughs varied considerably in their demographic composition. Metborough was ethnically mixed with over a hundred different languages spoken in its schools and more than a thousand refugees in its secondary schools (around 12% of the school population). One very distinctive feature of Metborough involved the mobility of its inhabitants and the sharp contrasts of wealth and poverty in close proximity. Post-16 education provision in the borough was covered by seven comprehensive schools, two Further Education colleges, and many young people crossed borough boundaries both pre- and post-16. There were also 11 independent schools in the borough. Work-based learning was restricted to the two colleges and only one private training provider, although there was a range of other providers in adjacent boroughs within reasonable travelling distance.

Reaching agreement to bid to be a lead body Connexions Partnership was a major achievement given such a large number of local authorities involved. The boroughs differed greatly in the problems they faced, their political complexion and their reputations for public services. The chief executive (appointed in the summer of 2002) was a local manager of one of the pilots that took place in the separate boroughs in 2001-02. He was therefore very knowledgeable about the areas in which the Partnership operated.

Like the other models, Metro Connexions had a Partnership Board and several LMCs covering each of the local authorities. One key feature of Metro Connexions that received favourable comment from stakeholders was the way in which service planning was based on ideas developed by each of the area LMCs and the strong links between these and the central strategic Partnership team. This central team was also supported by the lead body authority through service level agreements with its key departments. Apart from these agreements, Metro Connexions contracted for front-line services with a number of different providers. In this sense it was a variant of the subcontracting model rather than a direct delivery model of Partnership delivery. The main contract holders included career companies delivering mainstream careers education and guidance services to schools and colleges, as they were doing prior to the arrival of Connexions, together with the constituent local authorities.

In Metborough there were 14 PAs employed by the careers company and a further 22 employed by the local authority Youth Service. According to estimates of the size of the cohort, this gave a higher PA to young person ratio than in either of the other two areas covered by the research. In Metborough the ratio averaged around 1:300, compared with 1:455 in Midland Connexions and 1:550 in Nortown.

During the course of the research, and following a consultant's report, the PAs not employed by the careers company became reorganised into three discrete teams, each with a manager responsible for the day-to-day supervision and support of the team. One of the teams offered extra support to schools, another supported the One-Stop-Shops and the third was a group of six PAs operating in a number of specialist settings: City of Metborough College, the Housing

Assessment and Advice Centre, Medical Centre Children with Disabilities Team, the YOT, a Language Support Unit, and the Leaving Care Team in the social services department. Starting in 2004, Metro Connexions began a special project funded by the European Social Fund aimed at reducing the number of young people who were NEET. This enabled access to special funds of up to £1,000 per person on the project to help overcome barriers to work or training. There are similarities between this and the participation trial operating in Northern (see below).

Northern Connexions and Nortown

Northern Connexions Partnership was large, complex and covered around 180,000 young people aged 13-19 drawn from a number of different local authorities. The chief executive was appointed in the spring of 2002 and the Partnership started operating for the first time in the autumn of the same year. Nortown was considered by the Chief Executive Officer of Northern Connexions as one of the biggest challenges. It had around 50,000 teenagers, spread across a large city, a number of small towns and a large rural area – three quarters of the district was classified as rural. The district had clusters of young people from minority ethnic groups, constituting around one third of the school population. Nortown also had one of the lowest educational achievement rates in the subregion and some of the highest NEET rates.

The Partnership was seeking to promote multiagency work across the subregion through the issuing of multiple contracts to a variety of different service suppliers in the different local authorities. In each LMC area the major contract holders included a careers company, the LEA, the Youth Service and voluntary sector bodies. The Board also supported a national pilot initiative funded by the national Learning and Skills Council – a one-year participation trial. This programme focused on support of a number of target groups including young people who were NEET and those at risk of dropping out from post-16 learning. This was done through support from Key Workers, directly employment by the Partnership. As well as working with a small and targeted caseload, Key Workers could also access funds to help, support and reward young people's participation, and where necessary, their learning or training costs.

The major contract in the city of Nortown was with Careers Nortown, a private careers company. This funded a total of around 60 full-time equivalent PAs, most of whom were working in mainstream education and were school-based. Careers Nortown PAs also included a 'Community Team' composed of seven PAs from a variety of disciplinary backgrounds. It also managed one PA seconded to the Independent Living Team working with care leavers and young people who were homeless. Another PA was seconded to the local YOT. These latter contracts were not issued until August 2003, so working practices and caseloads were not well established. Contracts for other specialist PAs were delayed until late in 2003 and early 2004 due to difficulties in identifying and agreeing on their deployment.

From the early planning stages there had been reluctance across Northern to accept the need for Connexions to be organised on a subregional basis. Those involved had hoped that the subcontracting partnership would allow for very significant delegation of authority and control to LMCs but the chief executive saw things differently. The first two years of the Partnership at Board level had been a site for conflict and acrimony, a reminder that forced collaboration between agencies can sometimes occasion antagonism, bitterness and dysfunctionality as well as cooperation, harmony and partnership. A number of different areas of grievance emerged. These included a perceived lack of consultation on the content of the second business plan, poor coordination of efforts in the contracting and deployment of the outreach facility, the direct employment of Key Workers under the participation trial, the need for a subregional computer system, and the long delays in the development of contracts to cover the full complement of PA posts across the districts. Many of those interviewed hoped that the conflict that was a feature of the first two years of the Partnership Board had come to a close. But it is worth noting that, as the fieldwork for the research was concluding, a further round of antagonism took place around proposals for dealing with a VAT bill crisis, and the possible reversion to a lead body arrangement.

As we will see in subsequent chapters, when partnerships are not clearly signalled from the leaders of agencies and organisations, and re-enforced by agreements on joint working, this can have serious consequences for front-line workers. The next chapter examines interagency work taking place in the three partnerships by taking three case studies of young people with whom Connexions PAs were working.

Change over time

Finally we should add a word of caution. The Partnerships in the study have been developing their structures and patterns of working throughout the period of the research, making any static description of the 'current' state of affairs problematic. For instance, the fieldwork for the case studies took place between autumn 2003 and spring 2004. Some of the data collected is, at times, negative about the practice relationships between partner agencies. As is common in the research process, these situations will have changed, and may have improved, since the data was collected. Our intension is to describe the situations as we encountered them so that more general lessons can be drawn by all Partnerships for the future development of the service. In order to capture the dynamics of change, the chief executives of the three Partnerships were interviewed on several occasions, including an opportunity for them to comment at the end of the project after they had read an early draft of this report. We were pleased to learn that many of the areas we had identified as areas of weakness in the initial draft had been ones they had also identified and spent considerable time and effort in attempting to remedy in the months following our initial fieldwork.

2

Three case studies of work with young people

In this chapter we provide a detailed description of three case studies, one from each of the research areas, so that the reader is familiar with the detail of some of the cases in which interagency work is taking place, as well as being introduced to the 'inevitably messy' contexts of interagency intervention and partnership. One of the important features of the design of this research was in linking interviews with key stakeholders with individual case studies. The former gave insight into the strategy and local planning of Connexions, and the latter an opportunity for a detailed examination of interagency work in practice.

The overall selection of the cases to include in this project differed slightly between the three research areas, with different Connexions 'gatekeepers' being used to recruit PAs who were willing to take part. In all areas the same template of 'case types' was employed so that we could explore how the different Partnerships worked with YOTs, care leavers, young people with special educational needs and other interagency contexts. The inclusion of a case always depended on the young person explicitly giving 'informed consent' to taking part in the research (and, in the case of young people under the age 16, we also obtained parental consent), and also agreeing to an 'information sharing' protocol for the purposes of the research. All young people taking part were promised anonymity and are referred to here by a pseudonym. Some young people chose a new name for themselves; others have been renamed in the interests of confidentiality. All young people taking part received a gift in recognition of their contribution to the project.

Sal (Midland Connexions)

Pre-16 negotiation of responsibilities and barriers

Sal lived in the Midland Connexions area and was an intelligent and bright young person who had a history of intermittent attendance at school. She was referred to a Connexions PA following a disclosure to a member of staff at a youth centre. The PA was located in the Community Education (Youth Service) team, housed in the Youth Office where the youth centre/club had its venue. It transpired that Sal's attendance at school had been patchy since the age of 14, for varying reasons. Latterly she had been experiencing panic attacks. At some point, Sal's school had referred her to the local social services department, owing to concerns about her lack of attendance, and what was potentially happening at home. Despite this, it appeared that social services were not expressing concern about what was taking place, although it was a matter related to potential physical abuse by the boyfriend of Sal's mother.

The PA took up the case when Sal was in Year 9, that is, 14 years old. Sal's mother had received letters about non-attendance, and had been 'threatened with Court'. The PA arranged with Sal to meet her in school and talk about some of the reasons for her not wanting to attend. By liaising with the Head of Year at the school, an agreement was made to allow Sal not to go into some of the non-exam lessons that she clearly did not want to attend, with the intention of securing attendance in other subjects, and making better use of her time in school. There had also been discussions about a semi-work experience package, but this could not get off the ground as Sal was not yet in Year 10, a prerequisite of such packages. At the time, the PA was encouraged by the school to spend time there, mainly in topping up Sal's motivation to attend.

At that time, Educational Social Workers (ESWs) were school-based, that is, responsible for certain schools, and the PA worked with the school's ESW, encouraging Sal to attend. This relationship was found to be mutually beneficial, and for a while the work paid off, with Sal's attendance improving. When Sal entered Year 10, the Head of Year agreed to Sal embarking on work experience, and a placement at a local hairdressing salon was secured by the PA for one or two days a week, subject to Sal continuing to attend school. Sal was very excited about this. However, following a change in school personnel, the PA received a letter from a school management group questioning the PA's involvement and overturning the Head of Year's decision, stating that he had not been empowered to make decisions of this kind. The management group wanted Sal to return to lessons, as other young people might think they "could have it [work experience] as well". So Sal was told that she was not allowed to do work experience, and her attendance at school dropped again.

On the occasions when Sal did attend school, she was finding it increasingly difficult to cope with being there. The Head of Year 11 questioned the involvement of the PA and was reported to have said "it may be best if you didn't see Sal in school". However, at this stage the ESW stepped in and made a formal referral to Connexions to ensure the PA's continuing involvement. They worked together, making home visits to identify difficulties and discuss problems with both Sal and her mother. It emerged that Sal was experiencing high levels of panic at school, feeling confused and distressed by ringing bells and the rushing environment.

The PA and ESW negotiated with the school to agree a plan. The school preferred that Sal take work into the library at school, rather than doing it at home, although Sal said that no work was set for her, and she felt she was wasting her time, sitting in the library doing nothing. In addition, the school were not satisfied that Sal was experiencing panic attacks, and wanted evidence of this. In association with a GP and Sal's mother,

a referral was made to a psychologist. Sal's mother's relationship with her boyfriend had broken down, and she and Sal moved to a village with a high level of unemployment and a reputation for having little to occupy young people. The mother was dropping Sal off at school on her way to work, but Sal was unable to cope there, telephoning her grandfather to say how distressed she was. Soon after, her PA reported that Sal had "actually got to the stage then when she wouldn't even leave the house". The psychologist diagnosed agoraphobia. The school finally agreed to send work home for her, but Sal's mother claimed that no work arrived. Sal became increasingly depressed, and was taking medication for this.

She was referred by the school to a council-based special service, Education of Children Out of School (ECOS). The ECOS worker wanted Sal to remain on the school roll in case things did not work out with ECOS provision; the school would therefore continue to have a duty to educate her. At a review meeting between the PA, ESW, ECOS and a member of school staff, a package was agreed in conjunction with school.

During the school holidays Sal improved in health, and had managed to get herself out of the house. She had a boyfriend, who was quite a bit older and who seemed to the PA to be quite controlling. After the holidays, Sal was unwilling to return to school and her mother was in agreement. With these considerations in mind, the PA took the lead in discussing an alternative package with the school, who agreed to the PA investigating what this would encompass. A nearby college, which was experienced in working with Year 11 pupils with issues which prevented them from attending school, presented an attractive option for Sal. She was convinced that this would provide her with an opportunity to "have an education". Sal attended meetings where she described her history and took an assessment test, which she passed with a good score. The college agreed that Sal could start there with the new intake of Year 11s. The school told Sal that they would "write a letter" to her, and requested details as to course costs, which the PA obtained across a variety of scenarios according to the levels of support provided or agreed. The PA and ECOS worker were delighted that a flexible package had apparently been secured. Sal was committed to making a new start, enthusiastic about the options provided, and confident that she would be able to cope in a less bustling environment.

The day before the end of the school term, prior to the summer holidays, the PA received a brief fax from the school, listing several points. The fax noted that the school was unwilling to fund the college course, that they needed more details about the course itself, and if Sal was able to cope with college, she should be able to cope with school; she should therefore attend school for two days a week. The status of the referral and thereby the PA's involvement was again also questioned. The PA telephoned the school to point out that if final decisions were to be taken at the beginning of the next term, Sal would be missing the beginning of the year but, according to the PA "they just basically said 'no'".

Coinciding with these events, Sal's mother contacted the PA to say that Sal was acting strangely and she was worried about her. The PA became involved in supporting Sal's mother, as it transpired that, under the influence of her boyfriend, Sal had started to use drugs. Events spiralled, and Sal, then 15 years old, went missing for six days, during which time neighbours had seen her "squealing around the village" in her boyfriend's car. Sal's mother telephoned the social services department, who told her to call the police. The mother's house had been "ransacked" and she was increasingly frightened. When Sal and her boyfriend eventually turned up at the mother's house, Sal was bruised, in a drugged state and "hysterical". The boyfriend assaulted the mother, who was afraid to call the police at first, but later was persuaded to do so by the PA. A neighbour intervened and was threatened with a knife by the boyfriend. Sal and the boyfriend disappeared again, leaving Sal's mother very fearful and feeling that she would not be able to control Sal should she return. At this point the PA contacted social services, who said that they did not think there was anything they could do. When pressed by the PA, who put in writing her concerns for Sal's safety, social services responded with a letter:

> "Then I got the letter to say that [reading] 'Dear Maureen, I'm writing to let you know that following a consultation with my manager, it's been decided that social services will not continue with

involvement. Sal turns 16 next week and is already involved with a large number of agencies, it's not felt there is anything which social services could usefully add, I will therefore be closing Sal's file at this office'."

While Sal was still missing from home, her boyfriend was arrested for burglary. He was also charged with abducting a minor, as it turned out that he was 25 years old and Sal was under 16. The police took Sal back to her mother's house. Sal's mother phoned the PA (using a mobile phone number), as she was at a loss to know what to do with Sal, who was screaming, abusive and violent. The PA, who was away on holiday at the time, arranged for another Connexions worker to advise her. An appointment the following day with that Connexions worker did not happen, owing to the worker's difficult personal circumstances on the day. At this point, the PA referred Sal to an Alcohol and Drugs Advisory Service (ADAS) worker, who succeeded in working very closely with Sal. He shared limited information by keeping the PA informed on Sal's progress, but without disclosing details.

Sal's mother felt she was unable to cope with her, and so Sal moved to live with her grandparents. By this time her boyfriend was in prison, although Sal visited him every weekend. While Sal was still referred to ECOS, her mother contacted the PA to say she was continuing to get letters from the school threatening prosecution for Sal's non-attendance there. With the mother's permission, the PA contacted the school and ECOS to explain the situation. ECOS 'closed her file' (and ceased working with Sal) until her drug situation had improved. But they reopened it when Sal was feeling better, and was starting to want to "do something". An online learning package was agreed, although this was slow to start, as further agreements as to how this would be financed and practically arranged were not simple to achieve. The PA felt:

> "... angry that she's a young person, I think, [who] if she'd been in another school from Year 9 it would be a different story. It's just this one school has poo-poo'd ... everything that we've tried to do to move her on or to deliver an incentive there's been, they've gone along with it and then they've cut it dead. And it's sort of like they're not

keen for anyone to be involved or question what's happening here."

Sal's feelings were:

"It gets me angry that they tell me something, tell me one thing and they don't do it, you know. So each different person's come out and told me they're going to do something for me and they haven't and then it makes me lose interest. I think, 'Well why should I do it? If you can't be bothered why should I bother?'"

Aged 16 at the time of the interview, she expressed a quiet understanding of the efforts her PA had made on her behalf:

"She tries but then someone else higher above her or whatever tells her that it can't happen, so you can't really have it."

The PA remained optimistic that Sal could be found a work experience placement prior to the boyfriend's release from prison, to enable Sal to achieve some independence and motivation for herself, and gain some sort of qualification.

Key questions

Sal's case study illustrated some of the inherent tensions Connexions workers had to face in working across institutional barriers. Her PA was trying to ensure that Sal got the best out of her pre-16 education, but Sal's school had not always appreciated the intervention being planned, and on more than one occasion had vetoed it, refusing to give the financial support necessary. It must be emphasised that this degree of hostility and lack of cooperation is not usually encountered. This case study does raise some serious *structural* and *systemic* issues about the capacity of the Connexions Strategy: can it fulfil its aims without the cooperation of key partners? And what can be done with them to secure a more effective partnership?

In Chapter 3 we detail evidence that suggests that one of the key ways in which PAs build trust and rapport with young people is being able to promise and deliver services others have failed to give. If other partners delay, deny or obstruct the services being made available, then that not only

affects access to the services themselves, it undermines a relationship of reliability and trust. Part of the skill involved in partnership working is to be able to effectively negotiate and 'broker' services. Where services and obligations are not being provided or fulfilled, part of the PA's task is to act as an 'advocate' for the young person in ensuring that partners deliver them. Some of the 'brokerage' and 'advocacy' can be ensured by senior stakeholders at Board or LMC level, or through agreements between senior managers of partner agencies. Yet some has to be carried out by PAs in their daily dealings with schools, school managers and others. What Sal's story illustrates is that such partnerships may well run into differences in perceptions of the issues being addressed, conflicts of interests, and basic differences in cultures of responsibility between agencies who are charged with working together.

Tariq (Northern)

Connexions at the margins and too little information sharing?

Tariq's family were of Pakistani origin and at the time of the research he was 17. He lived with his parents and his two (older) sisters and a younger brother. His mother did not work and his father was 'long-term unemployed', so the family had no income other than benefits. Tariq was first referred to the Connexions community team in December 2002. His PA contacted the Youth Offending Team (YOT) to let them know she would be acting as his Connexions PA.

Tariq's YOT file indicated that he had been involved in a street robbery in a neighbouring town and given an eight-month Detention and Training Order in a Young Offender Institution (YOI) in 2002. It indicated that the robbery for which he was sentenced had been undertaken with a friend during the period when Tariq was taking his GCSEs. He had had the day off for revision between exams and had gone to see his friend in a neighbouring town. Here they had forced another young person to give them around £5. Tariq's friend had a replica gun tucked into the waistband of his trousers. They had shown the gun to the victim. There was CCTV tape of the area in which the robbery took place and both were later arrested as they were using the money to play on slot machines (gaming machines) in an arcade in the next town. His YOT case worker became involved between his conviction and the sentence and was involved in preparing the pre-sentence reports.

His YOT worker did not undertake the initial assessment of Tariq himself but referred to the standard assessment (ASSET) on file. The assessment had involved a home visit as well as one-to-one interviews with Tariq. He was described as "having a lot of problems at home", and his father as "a strict disciplinarian". When we interviewed him, Tariq said his parents were upset at his arrest and his father had beaten him.

> "Got battered. It's life innit! If I didn't get battered that violently, I would have done it again every day."

His YOT worker says that, at home, Tariq is seen as a "really polite young man" but outside with his mates he liked to present a more glamorous image of himself:

> "I think he likes to show he is 'one of the boys' and he wants a lot of 'street cred.'… 'I am Tariq; I've "my boys'."

This was something about which his YOT worker had continuously challenged him.

Tariq had done quite well in his GCSEs; he had obtained nine passes, although not particularly good grades. Tariq said he was disappointed, although, in his YOT worker's view, he had done as well as could be expected. Tariq wanted to become a car mechanic and had initially registered at Nortown Further Education College before the offence took place. There is uncertainty about whether he ever started the course because of his impending trial, but his imprisonment and consequent lack of attendance led to deregistration in February 2003.

After Tariq had been sentenced, his YOT worker had arranged an initial Detention and Training Order meeting at the YOI. This had involved YOI staff, his YOT worker, Tariq and his parents, and they had agreed a 'care plan' mainly focusing on his education and training needs. It also involved a 'MORE' course – Motivating Young Offenders to Re-think Everything – and a victim awareness course. Tariq was not able to take a course on motor vehicle maintenance as all places were filled, mainly by offenders likely to serve much longer sentences. The courses he did take involved 'fixing TVs' and 'electrical wiring' as well as Mathematics, English and IT. His YOT worker said that Tariq was shocked by the conditions in the YOI:

> "When I initially saw him he was very frightened. The whole experience was new to him. It was nothing like his expectations…. And I think that came as a big shock to him. And, when inside, he realised, 'This is not me and this is not my life' … when he was in prison he did NOT like it."

Tariq was released 'on tag' (electronic surveillance and a curfew) after three months, with the Detention and Training Order requiring him to complete the training part of his order while living in the community. However, almost immediately there was an incident, the details of which remain disputed. Tariq's version, which he told at the end of our interview with him, was as follows:

> T: "Bit nasty stuff happened. You know. My parents and all that…. After I came out of jail, then a few days later I did a mission again, didn't I? And then I was in police station and see my dad. And he flipped and the police station copper gripped him. And I legged it, whatever, back in my cell and locked myself in, and all."

Tariq told us that he had been caught after a car chase riding in a stolen car with a friend. His YOT file, however, indicated that he had been arrested with a friend for shoplifting sweets and crisps. What is not disputed is that, after his arrest, Tariq's father went to the police station. His YOT worker told us:

> "… his father turned up at the police station. And made threats like 'I am going to kill you. You have dragged my name through mud. And, you know, you have just come out of prison and you haven't learnt your lesson.' But I don't think his father was realising that Tariq was growing up, and he needs pocket money. And if you don't give him that, what is he going to do. And he wanted

to be with his friends. He smokes. And his father was not acknowledging these things."

The police wanted to release Tariq on bail but he refused to go home and emergency accommodation was arranged for him by the YOT in a local hostel. This was done by the duty officer as Tariq's YOT worker was not on duty when the events occurred. But on the Monday morning, both Tariq and his mother were waiting for him in some distress.

"And his mother broke down, and there are issues about domestic violence, and Tariq witnessed a lot of it. And he was saying, 'I am not going to put up with it any more'. And he's grown up, and he's going to charge his father with it. And obviously I'm advising her that she can put a complaint in.... But she said, 'No that's fine', and she wanted to go back home to her husband....

"But she was worried about Tariq going back home. She thought there was a genuine threat from his father to give him a serious beating. And from that conversation I gathered that Tariq has been through it before.... Tariq was crying, he was weeping, in front of his mother. Was literally crying when all this happened and he was so scared...."

On release, the YOT worker had also referred Tariq to a 'mentoring' project funded by the Youth Justice Board and working in partnership with the local YOT. The scheme also works closely with the families of Asian young offenders and involvement with the project starts with a home visit in which all family members are encouraged to be present. This is followed by a five-unit course for the offender based on cognitive behaviour therapy, followed by a 'residential' where the mentor is chosen. Tariq's mentor also worked as a 'learning mentor' in local schools, something he admitted had prevented him having as much contact with Tariq as he would have liked:

Interviewer: "How many times have you seen him?"

Tariq: "Never. Only at the bus stop when he's going to school. He goes and works at ... [girls' school].... He works up there. And then he goes in mosque – he's a Sufi, so its hard isn't it. He goes to the Mosque training, teaching kids at school. No time for me."

One of the managers at the mentoring project had proved instrumental in arranging a training placement. Since his release from the YOI, Tariq had been seeing a Connexions PA who had been trying to get him involved in a number of training courses. She knew he wanted to take a car mechanics course and had arranged one interview and test for him, but he had failed the test. She had then organised a course at Nortown College together with training at a local provider, but he had not turned up for interview. Time had passed and the college term had started when the manager from the mentoring project intervened on Tariq's behalf. He rang the college to confirm that the main course on motor mechanics was indeed full. But he managed to talk one of the tutors (a friend of his) into letting Tariq and Tariq's friend on to another course that involved learning-related practical skills such as welding. Both his Connexions PA and the mentoring manager kept in touch with Tariq's progress and found that he and his friend initially did much better than most others on the course. With hindsight, both wished that Tariq had gone on the course on his own, and not with his friend as they thought he was 'easily led'. There was an incident at college involving a security guard and one of the tutors. Both Tariq and his friend were excluded from college: Tariq for swearing, his friend for threatening the tutor and another member of the class. Tariq thought racism was involved in the behaviour of the class member, the tutor and the police when they were called. But he did not want either his PA or the mentoring scheme to intervene on his behalf.

Despite all this, Tariq's PA has continued working with him trying to give him a new start. At the time of our interview, Tariq had been spending much of his time at a local gym, out with friends or at his friend's house playing on computers. He still had ambitions to become a car mechanic and, after training, raising a loan and running a garage with his friend – but he has a long way to go. His PA fixed him up with an E2E course being run by the Youth Service, which Tariq thought looked promising:

"That's a proper place for youth offenders – swearing and that. The college don't like that. Because when you go to college they record every swear you say, every lesson. Mine had about 200 swears and all this and that. [But] that's the talk innit."

Tariq's YOT worker regarded Tariq as now "off their books", although his record remained on their computer system. This contained important information about his turbulent family life and the circumstances in which he had offended in the past. His YOT worker did not regard Tariq as a particularly difficult offender to work with, just a "bit of a softy", "easily led" and sometimes tempted to avoid the authoritarian nature of his family by entertaining fantasies of being a local gangster with "his boys". None of these 'judgements' were being shared with his Connexions PA. A different Connexions PA had been allocated to the Youth Offending Team and, as a member of the Team, had access to the information system. But this was not being shared with other Connexions PAs working with offenders, including Tariq's PA.

Tariq's Connexions PA seemed unaware of any issues concerning his home background. She was youth work trained and described herself as comfortable working with both the English and Pakistani communities. She thought that she got on with Tariq and he described her as "sound". But she thought it inappropriate that she should enquire into his previous offences or the circumstances in which these occurred or to probe too closely into his home circumstances. She had asked him about his home circumstances and he had told her there were "no issues". We also asked about whether a formal Connexions assessment (APIR) had been carried out with Tariq and about information sharing with the Youth Offending Team. An APIR had not been used with Tariq although, at the time of the interview, it was being used with new clients. She recognised that an ASSET assessment would have been made by the Team but this was not information that was yet shared with Connexions. As she explained:

"I think that eventually all these things will pass on. But because I think at the top they have not got all the agreements signed for information sharing, to be honest with you. 'Cos I've never been told or briefed that I am supposed to [pause] ask them for their assessment. It's not put in with the referral. So the systems are not really in place yet."

This PA was reluctant to be proactive in seeking out what might be relevant background information about her client, and this effectively restricted her role to that of, fairly narrowly conceived, careers education and guidance work.

Key questions

This, and other cases covered in the research, illustrates some of the potential problems involved when information is not shared between agencies. Whether Tariq's PA would have responded differently to his needs had she been aware of the content of his Youth Offending Team file is difficult to assess. Like other PAs in the study, she was reluctant to pry into issues her client had not willingly disclosed to her. This made any genuinely holistic assessment of his needs impossible.

Two other aspects of this case are interesting and important. First, interviewees gave very different versions of Tariq, his criminal activity, his family circumstances and his exclusion from college. Only one version is recorded on an electronic data base, in this case the Youth Offending Team system. One important element of most information-sharing protocols is the agreement of the subject that information about them can be shared. It would have been inappropriate in this research to have asked Tariq whether he would have been willing to have his file made available to his Connexions PA. Yet it is also clear that, when asked by his PA about any problems at home he chose not to reveal anything. Did his PA 'need to know' about the violence he and his mother suffered at the hands of his father? Should Tariq have been allowed to keep aspects of his family life 'private' and unexplored by his PA? Would a more rigorous use of the APIR Connexions assessment system necessarily have revealed these details? Would the transfer of Youth Offending Team records at the point of referral or later have led to a helpful, or obtrusively unhelpful, sharing of family secrets? Would Tariq have benefited from this?

Second, although the lack of information sharing in this case may well have been due to the slow development of information-sharing protocols in the Northern Connexions area, at the time of our research information was not being *systematically* shared between Youth Offending Teams and Connexions in either of the other two Partnership areas. In the case of Tariq, his Connexions PA also thought that such information sharing was inappropriate. Indeed there were other cases covered in the research (see Chapter 3) in which there were formal agreements with voluntary sector agencies that information about young people should *not* be passed on to Connexions. For information to be used systematically and effectively, therefore, requires much more than the establishment of a protocol. It requires that this be incorporated into agreed working practices in which PAs are trained, managed and supervised to ensure these are systematically followed. Some PA also need to be convinced (by both training and supervision) of the importance of information sharing and the use of APIR assessments.

A third point highlighted by this case relates to the different roles played by a Connexions PA and other professionals working with the same young person. In the case of Sal, discussed earlier, the PA clearly saw her role as champion of Sal's rights and key advocate of her welfare, despite opposition from others. In the case of Tariq, the Connexions PA was content to allow others to take the lead. Initially this was because a custodial sentence stood in the way of the development of Tariq's learning career. But she was also content for the mentor scheme manager to take the lead in brokering his post-release college course for him, because he seemed to have better leverage with the tutor than she did. She also concurred with his judgement about not intervening with the college when Tariq was excluded, despite suspicions about the possibility of a racist element in the incidents surrounding this. She seemed powerless to arrange another placement until the E2E training provider gave her a start date. In partnerships, some partners have to accept that they are junior partners. But this case does raise questions about how central the PA was as advocate for the promotion of the welfare of her client. Sometimes, however, always trying to play the lead role as a strong advocate can create difficulties for the PA, as is shown by the next case.

Sam (Metro Connexions)

A young carer with post-16 barriers to learning

The third case we examine is taken from the Metro Connexions area. The deployment of PAs in Metborough included a large team with the careers company largely delivering the universal service in schools and colleges, a specialist team working with schools, as well as those working in agencies such as YOTs and Leaving Care teams, and those working with One-Stop-Shops.

Sam was a 17-year-old white male who lived in a one-bedroom council flat with his 75-year-old father. His mother died a few years ago leaving Sam and his father living alone. He had an older brother who had his own place. He and his father had lived in the flat all of Sam's life. They managed by using the sitting room as a second bedroom. Sam had a 'guardian' who was a friend of his mother and who lived in a distant town. He sometimes spoke with her on the telephone and she visited him sometimes. While she was supportive she was not in a position to help him financially. He also had friends at a local Catholic church.

He attended a sixth form in "a good school" in Metborough, although Sam lived in a different borough covered by a different Connexions Partnership. As was made clear in Chapter 1, it was not unusual for young people to go to school in one borough and to live in another. Sam had done well academically in his 16-plus examinations, achieving nine A-C grades GCSEs and one D grade. He had been in contact with his Connexions PA for approximately one year. She was an ex-teacher and he was initially referred to her by his Head of Year because he was not able to complete successfully his first year in the sixth form. Sam's father was described as being 'infirm' and showed signs of dementia. Sam had cared for his father for some time without any support, doing what he could to look after the house, provide meals and took frequent calls from his father during school time, to the detriment of his studies.

> "He once called me six times in 15 minutes while I was in a lesson. And it could be quite testing because I have to try and be patient with him and it can be really hard."

Sam also had issues with his own motivation and with his own health, as he was quite overweight and there was concern about his diet and his ability to look after himself. It was clear that Sam did not have anyone else to look after him.

The only household income was Sam's father's pension/benefits, and so Sam had difficulty with money and making ends meet. At one stage he even struggled to come into school at all because he did not have the travel expenses. His father's pension money was often cashed by Sam's older brother who was said to have an alcohol problem (see below). Initially Sam was not thought to be entitled to benefits in his own right because he lived at home and was in full-time education. The first work that the PA did with him was to try to help him with money, helping him to apply for an Educational Maintenance Allowance (EMA). He eventually received this, back-dated for the whole academic year, and for a while things seemed to settle down. As the immediate problem of money was solved, contact with his PA reduced.

During his first year in sixth form (and after initial contact with the Connexions PA), there was also a violent incident involving Sam and his brother. Sam approached the local social services department (Children and Families Division) about this. He was seen by a social worker from the assessment and referral team of the borough where he lived rather than Metborough. With Sam present, the social worker telephoned the adult social services team about his father. He was advised to contact the police about the assault but declined to do so. In addition, the social worker contacted a Connexions One-Stop-Shop for benefits advice. But this again was in another borough and in a different Connexions Partnership area. Sam also approached the One-Stop-Shop but declared it to be "terrible". He said the staff there did not try to help him and did not even have the right (EMA) forms. His school PA also had no meaningful contact with his home Connexions area. Sam was not taken on caseload by social services but was invited to return in future if he felt the need to do so. He was disappointed with the lack of help he received from social services:

> "They just spoke to me and didn't offer any advice. They didn't chase up anything, which wasn't particularly good."

Sam's PA was employed by the Youth Service and was part of Metborough schools' team giving extra support to those with high levels of need. She asked her line manager, the school's Social Inclusion manager, whether she should get in contact with the social services team that Sam had approached, but was advised not to do so. The PA reported that her line manager said that it was the responsibility of the Social Inclusion manager to liaise with social services as child protection was part of her role. Sam's PA initially thought that he had an allocated social worker with whom he had been in contact, but after speaking with social services they denied this.

At the time of the research, Sam was repeating a year at school so he could take his AS levels again and, hopefully, get better grades. There was a problem with his EMA for the current academic year, insofar as the EMA department were asking for further documentation about his father's income and Sam was having difficulty obtaining this. His father was not able to engage fully with what was happening. Because of this, Sam was re-referred to the PA by his Head of Year. The PA tried to help with this by calling the EMA team in the borough where he lived. But they were unable to discuss individual cases (and because of this unable to say anything to the research team).

There was clearly a lack of 'joining up' of procedures and practices concerning the administration of EMAs, despite this being part of the Connexions Strategy. EMAs will be administered through a national body as of September 2004 and local authorities will cease to be involved. This change will not impact upon the problem of EMA staff being unwilling to discuss individual cases with PAs because of data protection issues.

> "They [the EMA team] know my dad can't do anything. They know I'm in full-time education but they still won't let me do anything over the 'phone without my dad there. I try to 'phone up with Sarah there and can't get anything done because my dad's not there. Data protection and all that – red tape. Sometimes I have to miss lessons just to 'phone up.... Most of the offices close at 5pm."

In the interim, Sam received some 'emergency funding' from Connexions, which was held by the careers company. This was similar to a hardship grant. Also, unknown to the PA, for a short time the school were giving Sam help with his travel expenses. She felt that no one was really taking a coordination role and this was being made worse by relationships within the school, and having to deal with different local authority areas.

> "I found out yesterday that the school was giving him travel allowance and I knew they were giving him travel allowance, but after I mentioned that I'd now actually got the fund, the funding from … Careers, my line manager said, 'Oh, well the school will put some money up as well. Just find out from the school'. And it's that kind of, nobody actually being, having an overall picture of what's happening.… And in my point of view, that is what a Connexions PA does. And it's a prime example of a case where that is absolutely vital, but it's, I think it's not happening because of various things."

Sam's father was soon due to move out of the flat and into sheltered housing. Sam said that social services had told him this was because he was not doing enough for his father. Sam was hoping to keep the flat and become the main tenant when he became 18. But there were questions remaining about how he would support himself and pay the rent. Sam should be entitled to Housing Benefit and Income Support as long as he is in full-time, non-advanced education if no one is acting in place of his parent. However, if he goes to university after this, he will be liable to pay full rent and council tax. At the time of the research he was receiving some support from his girlfriend's family, going to their house for meals and sometimes staying overnight. Ben hoped his girlfriend would move in with him if he got his own flat.

Most of the young people on the school PA caseload have issues with their behaviour. This is often the main reason why teachers and Heads of Year refer them. The PA said she was seen by the schools as someone who is there to sort out individual-based behaviour issues. This is quite a common perception in all areas, as we will see in the next chapter. Yet Ben did not have issues

with his behaviour and so, in this sense, did not present a problem to his teachers. As such, not all young people who perhaps should be worked with actually do receive attention. Ben was referred to the PA because his attendance at school started to be affected. Yet, interestingly, quite a lot of fixed-term exclusions occur at the school, but the PA is rarely involved. Indeed, a pupil being excluded does not mean an automatic referral to the Connexions PA.

At the time the research was undertaken, the PA did not think that her role within the school was clear, nor that the range of her responsibilities were particularly appreciated. She did not have her own room, and her desk was located in the staff room.

> "When I got to the school the Head had no idea what I was supposed to be doing and neither did my line manager. I think they like it on paper, they like to be able to say to people, this is the support we provide for students who are having difficulties. But in practice, I would say, 75% of the senior staff are actively against the work that I'm trying to do."

She felt that there is quite strong organisational opposition, as she explained:

> "Connexions really is a youth agency as opposed to an education establishment. I think they find their own values very threatened by Connexions' ethos of listening to young people and young people being at the heart of something. Whereas, although I think it probably should be the same in schools, it's not. And it can't be, because of the way the system is. And it just doesn't, it doesn't work together … they don't want someone coming in from Connexions with all the Connexions-speak."

The PA did not feel part of any wider Connexions Strategy, trapped as she was within a school environment. She reported feeling that, since she was a teacher, she had taken "three steps back" professionally in terms of the respect she was given within a school environment and the level of responsibility and autonomy she had.

"I think because I work full time in a school I'm really removed from the rest of the service. I feel really removed ... certainly the ideas and the aims and objectives of Connexions sometimes don't seem to fit with what I'm doing here. I feel like I'm more part of the school than part of Connexions. And I feel like my work is controlled by the school rather than by the aims of Connexions. So there's that – always a tussle between what Connexions is aiming to do in my role and what the school wants me to do and the things aren't marrying together, they just seem to be worlds apart really."

This gave rise to concern over who she was actually pleasing, if anyone:

"I'm never quite sure if I'm doing the right thing by the school, by Connexions or by the young person."

There was a learning mentor at the school but the roles of the PA and mentor had been separated rather than joined up. The mentor worked with Years 7, 8 and 9 and the Connexions PA worked with Years 10 to 13. Clearly Connexions work is intended to be with young people aged between 13 and 19, but the PA feels that there are other reasons for this distinction:

"I have turned into a learning mentor for the older ones."

Continuity of Connexions support during school holidays and when young people leave school was also an issue for school-based PAs, as were referrals between the different teams and other Connexions-sponsored activities. One of these is the Positive Activities for Young People's (PAYP) programme, mainly leisure and sports-based activities particularly designed to work with those at risk of disengagement. There were some referrals from the school PA to PAYP where young people meet the PAYP criteria. Also, PAYP tends to be group activities, therefore referring on to PAYP does not necessarily mean continuity of one-to-one support.

Key questions

Although there are some similarities to the issues raised by the first two case studies, Ben's case shows a lack of clarity in terms of the definition of the role of the PA, particularly when they are working in organisations which are not their own. There are also issues concerning the levels of responsibility and autonomy accorded to different professional workers, and the impact on the morale of PAs when their best efforts are baulked by others. It further raises issues of where such problems of interagency working may be best resolved and what tactics managers could adopt in trying to forestall the frustrations of front-line workers. In this case, none of the usual strategies for coordinating efforts, such as the calling of case conferences between all the workers involved, were attempted.

This chapter has introduced multiagency work under Connexions through three case studies. We have intended to give the reader a flavour of the day-to-day challenges faced by Connexions PAs when delivering the aims of the Strategy. The next chapter builds on the case studies and stakeholder interviews in order to examine the key issues thematically.

3

Issues and challenges in interagency working

The case studies discussed in Chapter 2 raised some fundamental issues about the problems and challenges of interagency working. This chapter draws on interviews with key stakeholders and case studies in order to analyse a range of those issues. In addition to focusing on analysis, the chapter provides insight into the practical challenges being faced by Connexions PAs and fellow professionals in their daily lives. We also focus on some of the main mechanisms through which interagency work takes place, and how these interface with the working relationships PAs have with young people.

Much of this chapter is concerned with the particular means, procedures, mechanisms and roles through which interagency working takes place. This includes how referrals are made, the sharing of assessments and information, as well as the distinctive roles played by Connexions PAs while acting as supporters and advocates to young people when involving other agencies. We begin by discussing the ways in which the size and shape of interagency networks are determined, and the level at which Partnerships foster and develop different sorts of frameworks.

Determining interagency networks

As pointed out in Chapter 1, some of these networks are determined nationally. This is signalled by the number of Cabinet Member signatures on strategy documents, and by the guidance given to Partnerships about the composition of their Boards and LMC. This indicates the sorts of institutional parameters that should be covered by interagency work under Connexions. The presence of some agencies represented at a Board level did not mean that the strategies agreed by the Board necessarily

would be implemented. Understandably, one head teacher on a Partnership Board cannot deliver the cooperation of all schools in the subregion. Representation on a Board by a chief executive of a strategic health authority did not mean necessarily that all the relevant health services were committed to interagency working with Connexions. A single senior police representative could not automatically deliver good working relationships between Connexions and the Youth Justice System. Many Board members did *not* have channels with which to communicate with their constituency or organisation about Connexions, nor did many see it as their duty or function to do so (see the Appendix).

Two other levels are of crucial importance in building the frameworks within which interagency work takes place. The second layer concerns the functions, through senior managers, of the range of services that are potentially involved. Careers company chief executives, YOT managers, social services managers, Youth Service managers, Teenage Pregnancy coordinators, head teachers, college principals and heads of student support services, together with the managers of some voluntary sector projects, are each crucially important in a number of ways. These include signing up their agency to partnership agreements, or protocols of joint working, or information sharing. Some of this might be facilitated by, or even through, LMCs, although many members regarded meetings as an opportunity to conclude and confirm previously agreed arrangements rather than as an occasion to initiate them. Responsibility for much of this second-level development of the network, therefore, rested on the ability of the Connexions local manager to negotiate with the appropriate agencies. The importance of this should not be underestimated and, of course, building these networks takes time. Yet it is often only through the managers of services that working practices and expectations can be established. Without clarity at this level, the nature of activities which front-line workers carry out routinely cannot be formalised as 'required', as distinct from being 'tolerated'. If overt recognition of role expectations has not been identified, it is PAs themselves who have to deal with the consequences, as will be illustrated later.

The third layer in determining networks is through the activity of the front-line workers. Even without the stipulations of a National Unit, or formal protocols and/or partnership agreements locally, front-line workers will develop informal networks with people they know and with whom they have worked. These informal networks are vitally important and must be recognised as such. They are not, however, the basis on which a secure and stable platform for interagency working can be built. If one worker leaves, the network may well be lost. But sometimes such informal networks can be encouraged, fostered and supported by more formal arrangements at the other two levels. Indeed, all the different levels have the capacity to re-enforce each other. Mandatory training for PAs, for instance, may give people the tools through which effective interagency working might take place. But many of the PAs we spoke with argued that the most valuable aspect of their training experience was in meeting others from adjacent agencies and learning about the work that they did. The relationship between all three levels is illustrated by a participation trial Key Worker in Nortown (see page 55) who spoke of her baptism of fire into her new job:

> "The first two months has really been networking and promoting the role because there is politics ... particularly in Nortown around the Key Worker role ... I think there's been a lot of animosity around the Personal Advisers particularly.... There's been quite a lot of back-stabbing I think, yeah, you know. And so it's kind of like having to break down professional barriers because you're working with people from other organisations who ... I think firstly the whole Connexions Strategy's not got its message across. People like schools still, see, they've got a careers

person in post. What's Connexions, who are you, why are you here, you know. I just think the message hasn't got out there to other partnerships, really."

The basis of effective intervention: building a relationship of trust

At the heart of effective working with young people is establishing a good working relationship. Sometimes this is based on the worker making a concerted effort to get to know the young person, or trying to engage with them in informal settings. At other times the worker simply may have to wait for the young person to tell them things that may be important, but will not be shared until the worker has gained the young person's trust. As one PA said:

> "I do think the quality of the relationship is, well it's crucial really. And so I do try and invest a lot of energy in that, 'cos that's going to sustain us through all the ups and downs...."

At times it was a matter of being able to do things for a young person that others were unable or unwilling to do, such as physically taking them to an appointment at a hospital:

> "It makes the young person feel better about themselves as well. You're not doing it just 'cos it's your job and you're getting paid for it."

Yet how is a good relationship with a young person established? One youth worker in Northern talked explicitly about it as a set of stepping-stones in which the first ones were crucial:

> "How do you build rapport? It's a million dollar question isn't it?... It's the nature of our relationship with that young person because we're non-threatening. It's never a teacher/student relationship.... But we're very non, non-judgemental of that, you know.... When that young person now feels that they can talk to you and sit there and tell you anything they want to tell you, that's when you know you've got rapport...."

"Well communication, they say only seven per cent is, is through words.... Ninety-three per cent of it's body language, you know.... So one of the things I do is 'match' ... it might be matching behaviours slightly, or mirroring their behaviours slightly. It may be mirroring the way they speak, using the words they use...."

"I'm from here, I'm from here ... I know young people in Nortown 'cos I was one myself ... and I know a lot of the needs of the young people in Nortown, I talk to them a lot."

"Humour's one of the most important things. If you can make them laugh you've won them over.... It's all on that first meeting. On the first meeting, whenever I meet a young person, I have to speak to them totally in private. But ... that's the moment when you catch them. If you don't get them then you'll never get them. You'll never ever get them."

Forming good relationships is a key principle avowed in all social practice settings. By remit, PAs occupy roles that extend beyond brief interventions, taking account of the wider contexts of young people's lives. Getting to know young people, respecting their choices and representing these is part of the process of relationship building. It provides space for young people to engage with potential opportunities, and for PAs to establish themselves as reference points offering continuity and stability.

But how are such relationships maintained within interagency working and how might they be helped by it? We turn now to the most frequent starting point in interagency work, namely, referral of cases from one agency to another.

Referral: procedures and processes

Part of the training that Connexions PAs and other co-workers undertake is on how the referral of young people to Connexions workers is best handled. Referrals may come from other professionals, parents or young people themselves, and are argued to be at their most successful when they contain information about the involvement of others, and where the work being done by other agencies is clearly documented. Efficient referral is seen as the foundation of effective interagency working within Connexions (Connexions, 2003a). In practice, however, such procedures are not always possible to observe, and many PAs said they had no alternative but to start to work with a young person where referral had been informal, with no accompanying paperwork and with little background being given by the referring agency.

Some referrals were based on something as simple as a telephone call from another professional. In Northern, perhaps because they sometimes expected to start work with individual cases as quickly as possible (to intervene in order to prevent a minor problem turning into a major crisis), participation trial Key Workers (see page 55) often knew little background to a case:

"I'm not sure they did have anything on paper. Sometimes we do and sometimes we don't. 'Cos we normally get it over the 'phone ... and to be honest, when I was new in post I didn't even know that there were special forms for referrals because nobody told us and nobody gave them to us.... You find out things bit by bit, by accident.... It would come to me by 'phone, yeah, ... I've written down here – 'phone call...."

In Midland Connexions, where practices were more fully developed over time, some PAs had started to resist referrals that resulted from informal contact with other workers:

"You could be walking down the corridor and you get a worker who'll say, 'I've got a young person, can you see them?'. You know, we've said 'There is a referral process and we have to stick to that'. It's like, if you're working in here you get YOT workers coming, in 'I've got a young person can you just have a five minute chat with them?'. We've had to say 'No, we can't do that, you have to put the referral in and do it properly'."

There was also significant variability between areas as to the likelihood of referral being accompanied by formal assessments. PAs working alongside a YOT in Midland Connexions were able to access the ASSET assessment:

"When we get a referral, attached to the referral is a pre-sentence report.... And we're also given a copy of an ASSET which is an assessment on the young person, so we have all that information, so we do work with it."

As we saw in the case of Tariq in Chapter 2, this was much less likely to take place in Northern. However, a PA in a different Midland Connexions team argued that referral and assessment necessarily had to be flexible:

"We all work very differently and perhaps because a lot of our work is practical and out and about.... Actually, sitting down and doing a load of forms is very low on our agenda. And also I'm privy to lots and lots of information and the ASSET assessment. And, we're not out to duplicate and to make a young person go through repeat processes and do things they've already been through. So I rely on the ASSET and speaking to the YOT practitioners to get a lot of information. And I also do a lot of assessment by observation."

Referral processes are often used dynamically to further the interests of young people, meeting their needs at given moments rather than being regarded as finite activities:

"They've been very careful about the Connexions role within YOT. They see it as a strength, the fact that I'm a voluntary intervention, and the young people, you know, they're encouraged to come and see me ... and if they miss an appointment I'll home visit, I'll 'phone up. I'll try and do what I can to keep them interested and wanting to, but there'll come a point where if they choose not to work with me, if they say they're not interested in the support and the opportunities that I can offer them, then it's batted back to the YOT worker to work on some of the other issues – why is this then, what's getting in the way of them wanting to engage with me, have they got some anger management, drugs, what's going on [pause] and I

think it's just a case of YOT then trying to keep me in the back of their mind and then make another referral, if and when they can."

At times, the fluidity required when referring to PAs or other agencies presented difficulties in terms of workload and its caseload management:

"They [referrals] come direct to us, so we have like a pigeon-hole with all our referrals in and we've got loads at the moment, so we've got, we've got about 20 young people each between myself and Gina, and that's a lot and it, you know, we're trying to dwindle the numbers down really, 'cos you can't do what you want to do with that amount of young people ... so the pressure's still on, but what we do, we look through the referrals and, you know, if it's an urgent case then we'd refer them straight to the One-Stop-Shop."

Identifying who might provide what kinds of services in order to suit the young person's needs at a given point was vital. This was frequently a matter for negotiation between different workers and agencies. At its best, a robust referral played a part in determining the start-point for appropriate work. Where referrals were less detailed or specific, considerable time was spent on 'getting up to speed' with why help was requested or expected by the referrer. In effect, work began afresh.

The flexibility in referrals into and out of Connexions conferred both advantages and limitations for interagency work. Where procedures were loose, it became difficult for PAs to determine or control the flow of their work, or the specific nature of it. Where insights into need, or more formal assessments, did not accompany referrals, the attendant lack of continuity for the young person required 'doing something' quickly. This, in effect, served to mitigate the gaps in communication. In cases where such gaps were apparent, PAs spent intensive periods of initial contact with young people that were positive, insofar as they helped to build necessary relationships. The implication here, however, is that workers did not necessarily benefit when referrals were formal: practice was not always accelerated.

What comes next? What do Connexions workers actually do?

In this section we comment of the variety of different roles taken by Connexions front-line staff and the different things they do. This covers their involvement in making detailed assessments of the needs of the young people they work with, brokering services of a range of other agencies and acting as advocate on the young person's behalf. Yet not all PAs fulfilled their roles in the same way. The final part of this section comments on the different roles they play and the impact this difference has on understandings and expectations of Connexions by those who deal with PAs in different circumstances.

Assessment of young people's needs

As we have seen, in some circumstances referrals came complete with an assessment by another agency and many PAs saw no need to duplicate the process. However, in other circumstances, assessment needed to take place. Connexions training recommends its own preferred means through which this is conducted (CRG Research, 2002). Within the training of PAs, the assessment and the planning of interventions is covered by APIR which seeks to give guidance on: how individual cases are assessed (A), activities planned (P), implemented (I) and reviewed (R). Not all PAs have completed all of the diploma training programme, although training in the use of APIR is now given through a separate training module (Connexions, 2003b). Since April 2004, APIR assessment has been mandatory for all young people with acute needs. The assessment part of APIR suggests that 18 different areas of need could, or should, be explored including: skills attained through education and training; family and environmental factors; issues concerning personal physical, emotional and mental health; and social and behavioural development including issues about motivations and attitudes. Assessment should explore a dimension from positive strengths to complex difficulties on each of the 18 facets (Connexions, 2004).

The APIR system encourages workers to use diagrams in their assessments. These indicate the intensity of needs in various different areas of review and subsequently allows the worker to plot any progress made. A PA in Midland Connexions explained:

"A lot of the young people I work with, everything would be in that critical bit in the middle – [critical and/or complex issues identified – inner ring]. And it's meant to be a visual guide to how they've moved on and they need to be moving on to be able to see some positives. So I think you have to be very careful how and when you used it. And the other thing is things like 'motivation' [is] one of the little sections. Well motivation's such a huge area and ... I'm not quite sure ... how useful that would be. And you'd have to know what area of motivation you were measuring that time to make sure it was the same area of motivation you were measuring next time, to be able to have a, some value in doing that."

Some workers were enthusiastic about the recommended methods of working, but nevertheless were wary of moving into a detailed 'formal' assessment too soon, lest it impact negatively on establishing a good relationship with the young person. Others regarded it as either common sense, or what they have been doing informally anyway. One participation trial Key Worker was positive:

"I mean from what I've seen of the training we did, it looks like, it looks like a very comprehensive assessment. I think it looks fairly positive 'cos you, you're going to adapt it with each individual young person. So you're not going to have to go into every, each of the 18 segments in detail if it's not appropriate. But I think anything that gives you a kind of tool and a guide is positive personally."

Another, less so:

"I mean, I realised when I did APIR, I thought, well this is just what I've always done anyway.... They accepted that the way particularly Key Workers are working, often, you know, you meet the kid in a cafe. There's no way you're going to sit there with an 18-page whatever and, you know, drawing on a sheet and, you know.... It might take you months to work your way through that process with somebody."

A youth worker in Northern was working mainly with young people either excluded from, or at risk of, exclusion from school:

"In order to get a young person to the stage where they're going to go through the APIR ... I think the APIR ... is fantastic. I'm really impressed by it. [But] the young people that we work with here, you're not going to get them into the Connexions office to sit there and go through that ... because it doesn't, they're not at that stage yet."

Other PAs thought that APIR potentially gets in the way and, as may be anticipated, some resented the time it took complete detailed information on potentially unwieldy or unreliable computer systems.

Brokerage and interagency work

Much of what Connexions does, in terms of interagency work, involves what the training material refers to as 'brokerage' (Connexions, 2004). Indeed the early calls for a new youth support service described it as a youth 'broker' (Bentley and Gurumurthy, 1999). What this implies is that, as well as listening to and assessing the needs of young people and agreeing on an appropriate course of action, the PA will then try to arrange for the delivery of an appropriate service from other service providers. Providers will, of course, differ according to the type of need being assessed, but typically may include housing and accommodation, benefits, specialist health or drug support, as well as a course in education, a training programme, an employment opportunity, or leisure services.

Brokerage often involved PAs in negotiating with different agencies with very different cultures and professional practices. Housing, Jobcentre Plus, and social services were cited by PAs in all areas as being *not* easy to deal with for a variety of reasons. For instance:

"I find housing the most difficult to work with. It's a number and because we don't

work in that style it's very frustrating when you're liaising with them because they just want a number and I hate working with them. It's not really their job to meet the needs of the young person, it's their job to house young people or adults but it's very impersonal. We're all about being personal."

Sometimes this was because the agencies in which PAs worked had their own rules, priorities and organisational constraints. Some PAs working in schools, for instance (as in the case of Sal in Chapter 2), found that senior management personnel could be hostile to the sort of work Connexions was trying to bring about. The Key Worker in Nortown quoted at the beginning of this chapter says she experienced hostility from both schools and from other Connexions PAs.

In Metborough, both Connexions and the Careers Service had 'One-Stop-Shops'. The one run by PAs employed by the Youth Service, however, did not have the relevant forms for young people applying for Jobseeker's Allowance under the Hardship Provision (ES9). At the time of the research, these were only available from the careers company within Metborough Connexionss.

Most of the PAs doing work other than careers education and guidance in mainstream schools were expected to be familiar with a wide range of patterns of local provision. This covered the 'welfare of young people' in its broadest meaning. As one of the PAs in Midland Connexionss commented:

"We have to know something about everything – whatever the topic might be, we might be called upon to know a bit about it, and for the whole of the city."

As far as education and training was concerned, sometimes this could be reasonably straightforward. But fitting together already existing patterns of provision to the assessed needs of the young person was not always easy. For instance, one common complaint was about the shortage of courses that could be flexible about start dates rather than insisting that everything and everyone must start in September. In some areas, however, there were also dire shortages of high-quality training. A youth worker in Northern, for instance, argued:

"... Having spoken to many of the PAs ('cos I attend a lot of their meetings) there isn't actually much in Nortown for the young people to do. Fine ... you do an assessment, you decide what best fits ... the category of this young person ... the modern apprenticeships. Most of them ... in Nortown have collapsed. There isn't actually anywhere for the young people to go. They're actually now telling young people you've got to try and get your own placement.... I mean it's, it's completely lost the plot, you know. There's only a very small percentage of young people who are actually getting back into it, you know, into E2E. There's nobody who wants to take on young people ... as apprentices."

If the places are not available there is little the PA can do, which of course potentially impacts on the quality of the working relationship.

Ensuring that young people attend interviews, register and attend their courses, or sit down to re-plan where things went wrong when they drop out, all forms part of the PA's work. Mick, in Nortown, was initially placed on a course in the city centre, but he left of his own accord because he was fearful of getting in with the wrong crowd. He had a conviction and was afraid these friends were enticing him into stealing again. His PA arranged a second college course in a neighbouring town that, again he left, because this time he thought he was getting too much homework. It was only when he was placed on an E2E course training in building skills which was nearer to where he lived that he seemed to be more settled. Choosing the right course, at the right level, with the right content, in the right place was something of an art form, especially when start dates could not be flexible. Furthermore, the suitability of courses was often tied to other facets of a young person's life, especially whether they were living in suitable accommodation and had sufficient support to maintain a work or study regime.

As with ensuring support in sustaining courses of learning, Connexions PAs spent a considerable time and effort supporting, checking and 'hand-holding' to ensure that accommodation needs

were met. One PA in Midland Connexionss explained the degree of support she tried to give:

"I can't attend tomorrow when he [another young person] goes for his accommodation appointment so I said to him 'Can I ring you?'. 'Yes.' So I'll make at least two 'phone calls to him tomorrow. I'll 'phone him at ten o'clock in the morning to make sure that he's on his way and then I'll ring afterwards."

Similar sorts of support were offered in the other research areas, especially to those deemed most in need. Robby, a black British care leaver in Metborough, was one young person with whom a PA was working intensively, with some contact at least once a week. In order to maintain this and to try and build his confidence, the meetings sometimes involved them playing squash or badminton together. The case, however, also illustrates some of the restrictions within which a PA must work. Like the other young people in the study who were leaving care and starting independent living, Robby was subject to the routine practices of the local authority. Until the age of 16 he had been brought up in foster care in a different borough. He had done quite well at school but not well enough to ensure he could take academic A-levels and be on track to fulfil his ambition to go to university as the offspring of his foster carers had done. Social services in Metborough often move young people back into the borough for independent living, as the PA explained:

"So young people go out of the borough when they're in care and then they turn 18 and we get them a flat. We fast track the council route and get them a flat that brings them back into [Metborough] because that's where we have to place them. So they leave their foster families, networks they've built up, maybe friends, maybe children of the carers. They leave all that network and move into [Metborough]."

After Robby had left his foster placement he had dropped out of a number of courses that had been arranged for him. Opinion differed between the various professional workers trying to help him as to the main causes of him dropping out. The linkage between accommodation problems and the ability to sustain learning placements was also an issue in Northern, as we will see in the next section. What is important to note is that some of the main barriers to being involved effectively in learning were structural rather than something that the workers or their managers could influence directly.

Advocacy: the PA as the 'powerful friend'

The work of Connexions PAs was not merely confined to putting young people in touch with services. Often to the most vulnerable young people, PAs became their 'powerful friends'. As one young person, Arnie, told us:

> "She [my PA] enjoys it [her work], she told us, so she's always got a smile on her face. Another good thing about Mel is if even if she's on her dinner break, like, I can get in contact with her, I can say, 'Mel, I need you' and even if she's on her dinner break she'll still come and see me, so she's pretty cool. Like I said she's not like a careers officer, she's more like a friend, a high-powered friend. She'll listen, that's what I like about her."

Arnie's situation showed a long history of contact with his PA, starting at a point prior to the existence of Connexions, when he was 14 years old and excluded from mainstream school. There had been various interventions with him, including outreach work in the community. At the time when he became involved with this research, Arnie was 18 years old, unemployed, claiming Jobseeker's Allowance and Housing Benefit, and living with his partner and three-month-old baby. During the time he had been in contact with Mel, he had greatly valued her support:

> "She's helped me a – well, a lot of the time, getting to training and stuff to get me back on track. I did have a sort of, well not a drug problem, but I was smoking a hell of a lot of cannabis, she got me off that, she helped me with that. I used to get in trouble with the law before because, like, everyone else had things and I didn't, so I was going out and getting them myself, and she basically helped me with that as well. She helped me at school, college."

PAs actively battling for their clients was illustrated in more detail by the cases of Sal (in Midland Connexions) and Sam (in Metro Connexions) in Chapter 2. As in these cases, advocacy could mean confronting a number of different agencies, something that requires considerable skill, courage and diplomacy. It was not always the Connexions PA who was best placed to fulfil this role. In three cases in the Northern research area, the role of advocate was taken by workers in voluntary sector projects, and in a further three the advocacy lead was taken by professionals other than Connexions PAs. What was important was that someone should be there to be the advocate and that the division of labour was clear and planned.

Benefits and/or entitlements to financial support were areas where workers not only gave advice, but often took a more proactive role to intervene on a young person's behalf. This was particularly important in the case of a young mother in Nortown. Mandy's PA had left Connexions to join Sure Start Plus when Connexions ceased to support the work the careers company was doing with teenage parents. Mandy was taking a full-time course at a local college while continuing to live at home with her parents. She continued her course after reaching her 29th week of pregnancy; indeed, she had her baby during the half-term break and continued her course after it, with own her mother looking after the baby. She had made three unsuccessful attempts to claim benefit from the Jobcentre and was on the edge of dropping out of her college course as she could not afford the travel costs. She had visited the Jobcentre Plus office on several occasions but was told repeatedly that she had no entitlement, or that her mother must claim extended Child Benefit. It was her Sure Start Plus worker rather than her PA who intervened on her behalf:

> "The under-18s at the Job Centre, are not young people friendly. And I knew they were wrong. So all I did was pick Mandy up, go down, tell them they were wrong. And she ... I made them fill forms in there and then and I made them write on the form, and she'd given this information to them and it needed backdating."

> "I've had young people having to write complaint letters, I mean in this job [Sure Start Plus] could do that on behalf of the

young person. I couldn't at Careers....
We weren't allowed 'cos of red tape and
politics at the top somewhere."

In Nortown there were plans for the co-location
of the Jobcentre Plus advisers working with the
under-18s and the Connexions One-Stop-Shop.
This was initially planned to take place in
January 2004 but had still not taken place by the
time the research ended, due to disputes with
unions about safety arrangements for their staff.

Although all young people in Nortown included
in the case studies had a Connexions PA, some
of them had only fleeting contact with them.
These included young people who had acute
needs. For some of these, advocacy was being
carried out by workers in the voluntary sector.
One case involved a charity supporting people
with disabilities who lobbied social services
(albeit unsuccessfully) on behalf of a young
person with special educational needs. He had
been at home (NEET) for a year at the age of 17,
being looked after by his mother and with no
contact from his PA. A youth worker, who was
working with a 14-year-old Asian boy with
special educational needs, intervened and called
a case conference after the boy disclosed that he
was being bullied at school and beaten at home.
His PA, who had a caseload of around 600 in a
mainstream school, had attended the case
conference, but had no other contact with him.

Repeated and persistent advocacy on behalf of a
young person was being undertaken by workers
at a voluntary sector project working with young
women thought to be in danger of being
groomed for prostitution. This involved
protesting when one young woman (Ghazella)
was returned home from care shortly before she
reached the age of 16. Later workers lobbied
social services on her behalf about unsuitable
(temporary bed and breakfast) accommodation
when she was returned to care, and later still
they tried to insist on the completion of a
'pathway plan' which had still not been agreed
nearly a year after her 16th birthday.

Like other 'looked-after' young people included
in this research, this young woman had a number
of different professional workers in her life all
trying to help her. But this case helps highlight
some of the problems in working together
effectively. Ghazella eventually obtained her own
flat but was worried about the implications this

had for the other decisions she had to make, her
ability to pay for it when she reached the age of
18, as well as what she should most sensibly do
in the meantime:

> "The maximum they will pay is £350. I've
> got to think about how I will pay for it
> once they stop paying for it in 2 years.
> I'm thinking shall I get into college now
> instead of thinking shall I get a job to
> pay for it. If I sort out my education now
> then I can get a better job to pay for it
> later."

With accommodation arranged, what should she
do next? And who was best placed to
understand her needs and advise her? Across
Connexions, social services and the voluntary
sector project Ghazella had numerous PAs and
Key Workers (a total of six). But there seemed to
be little planned divisions of labour between
them. There was some agreement of roles and
planned interagency work *within* a voluntary
sector team, to which Connexions made a small
contribution (one half day a week). But links
with social services and the Independent Living
Team seemed conflictual in nature rather than
predicated on principles of partnership and
cooperation, despite Connexions having a PA
located in both the voluntary sector project and
the Independent Living Team.

A confusion of different roles played by PAs?

What is clear in the three areas is that, despite
the generic title 'Personal Adviser', PAs perform
very different roles. In Metborough, at the time
of our fieldwork, a number of PAs commented
on the ways in which PAs employed by the
careers company and those employed by the
local authority were still operating separately and
had distinctively different approaches to their
work. Giving careers advice and guidance was,
of course, an important skill many PAs must
have, something many ex-careers officers were at
pains to tell us. Many PAs employed by careers
companies in Metro Connexions and Northern
are carrying out work in delivering what was
described to us as 'the Universal Service', very
different work from those carrying out more
targeted work. In schools and colleges many
professionals saw the same faces from the old
careers company doing what they thought was
the same job prior to the arrival of Connexions.

Yet many PAs saw their 'Connexions PA' role as very different from this. One in Metborough commented:

"It [careers and Connexions] is two separate things. Without a doubt it is. And, it will remain, I think it will remain that way because the careers staff are actually very different people. Careers people have got into that kind of work for a reason. And it's usually a quite different reason to why people in our [Youth Service PA] work, not just the way they get into it, but why they stay in it. They're much more bureaucratic than us. And they're much more regimented in the amount of time they spend and what they will do. And how much support they will provide. So to expect us all to be doing exactly the same thing, I think it's unrealistic. And a lot of them don't want to do it. They don't want to be a PA. But they have to be."

Many PAs working in schools, even special needs schools, were doing work that was largely the same careers education and guidance work done prior to Connexions. One head teacher of a special needs school was disappointed and exasperated by this, and the fact that this still failed to meet the needs of the case being discussed with him:

"Connexions in Nortown is just the Careers Service rebranded. I feel totally frustrated and fuming that all this money was supposed to be coming.... There is no difference to the way the services are delivered, it's just a change of label.... It [support from the PA for the case being discussed] should be someone within the school who knows him well ... able to discuss his timetable regularly and discuss with him what he needs – an individual timetable which could involve a mix of school, college, work, leisure needs, including outward bound courses.... We thought this was what Connexions was all about. Why can't they provide support workers/transitional workers to support placements ... and administrative support so they meet health and safety requirements?"

Among those PAs working intensively with a small number of young people there were significant differences in their deployment and approach being followed. Some PAs were attempting work 'generically' and 'holistically', in that they would assess and try and meet a whole range of needs that a young person might have. Others were sometimes placed as a single Connexions PA within another agency, working as part of a multiagency, interdisciplinary team dealing with client groups such as offenders or care leavers. Yet even where PAs were deployed in such settings (including those in voluntary sector), the work that they did depended very much on what others within the team defined as their roles. More often that not, even these specialist PAs seemed to restrict their work to giving advice on education, training or employment rather than more generic and supportive roles.

In Metro Connexions, support from PAs was at times arranged through a network established between different PAs who were each playing different roles. This was illustrated by the case of Kathryn who had a long-running dispute about housing with two different councils. Both initially refused to accept responsibility. Kathryn regarded her allocated college PA as her saviour – an advocate who had "made things happen" for her:

"The fact that Metborough have accepted me is all to do with [her PA]. It really is. The fact that she's been pushing for me to get in touch with them. The fact that she's been, just there, helping me. And she's liaised with them quite a lot, told them what's going on. And giving them information about me and stuff. She's just great."

The housing department that eventually helped her also had a Connexions PA located there. He was playing an influential role within the department in relation to his co-workers and ensuring successful outcomes for young people with whom he did not have direct contact. Yet this PA remained concerned about confusion of roles and duplication of effort:

"When I think about it, I've come across more problems of duplication within Connexions than between Connexions and other organisations."

While not all Boroughs had such a PA located in a housing department, this seemed to be providing a vital link in a network, ensuring that other PAs carried out their 'brokerage' work effectively.

In all partnerships, PAs were working as part of a team, although more integrated teamwork was more evident in Midland Connexions, the longest established partnership. Here there was most evidence of cross-referral between different workers:

> "We actually ask on the referral form what their status, what this young person's status is, do they have any assessments of any sort ... did they have any other professionals or services working with them which would tell us about drugs or sexual health ... the reasons for referral and what support is required for this person. And ... through that referral form we should be able to make a slight judgement or assessment to say, it's an emotional need, Jim could work with this. Or it's a careers need, Helen would work with this.... We're not possessive of our clients, but we're not there to say this is your client, that's your client, we are ... it's an open service and it's a cross-referring services. So our clients will have the input of the whole Connexions teams at some times, which will be focused in different things."

Establishing a skills mix within teams was, therefore, regarded as important.

Agreement on the coordination of roles and information sharing in interagency work

Working together as a team for the benefit of young people sounds an eminently sensible thing to try to achieve. But, as we have seen, it does present a challenge when the team is made up of different workers, steeped in different organisational traditions and cultures, with different qualifications and training backgrounds, and where work sometimes has to take place in different parent organisations and on their premises. Power struggles are not confined to boardrooms or council chambers. There are strong temptations for professional workers to defend well-established working practices and to

resent outsiders. As one of our stakeholders pointed out, effective partnership sometimes involved flexibility, modesty and a willingness to be led as much as an ability to lead:

> "They see us as good partners ... because we are flexible and we are prepared to be a partner where we're the junior partner. Now too many people are only prepared to be a partner if they're the lead. I personally took a view a long time ago when I said to them, 'You know, I want you to be valued as partners and that means on occasions, you know, you shut up and you don't say, yeah, we'll lead on this, we'll lead on that'. Because otherwise [it's a bunch of] leaders rather than being team players."

Divisions of labour and working together

Many of our case studies covered by this research involved a number of different professional workers working with the same young person. Nationally, no fewer than nine different documents have been produced about how agencies should work together and who should play the lead role as PA where the young person was dealing with several agencies at the same time (Connexions, 2002a-f, 2003a, 2003b). There were some instances in which networks seemed to be well-developed, flexible and effective.

The professional network surrounding Peter in Midland Connexions was relatively extensive. Peter was an unaccompanied minor, an asylum seeker from Kosovo, who had come to England in a lorry, accompanied by his cousin. Those working on Peter's behalf included a field social worker and his manager, an anti-drugs sports officer funded by the local authority, a specialist project Connexions PA located within the social services team, and a further Connexions PA responsible for training, based at a One-Stop-Shop. Peter was living with a foster carer at the time of being interviewed for our research. Each worker recognised that interagency working was functioning well on Peter's behalf, despite the awareness that he was not happy with his living situation, and was wanting to move to a town where his cousin was living. Each worker felt they were touch with the others, and each knew their respective areas of responsibility and therefore where each were likely to take a lead. All felt able to request a meeting to review progress and difficulties, and one such review took place as our case study was starting to take shape.

There were issues concerning Peter's age, which he claimed was greater than official records showed (under 16), and this had implications for his freedom to choose where he lived and make decisions for himself. The local authority had responsibility to foster Peter only within their own boundaries and proposed to review the situation when he turned 16. Those involved with Peter had seen him improve over a period of around two years, although all were aware that he was not happy. Peter did decide to move out of the area and went to live with his cousin. He was technically 'missing from care', although everyone was aware of where he was. His social worker and others had visited Peter and had decided that they would rather know that he was safe and where he was than force the issue by having the police return him to their local authority and run the risk of him disappearing. The Connexions specialist PA had referred Peter to the local Connexions Service where a PA, who had also worked with Peter's cousin, looked for opportunities to occupy Peter, as part of his vulnerability related to having no income and no school place. The Connexions staff were able to offer support regardless of local authority jurisdiction, and felt this to be a great strength in terms of continuity. Although, formally, Peter was 'missing', those with responsibilities for him were retaining their professional boundaries while at the same time ensuring that he did not 'slip through the net' and increase his vulnerability.

Under the subcontracting model one might expect that the terms and conditions of contracts themselves should make clear which roles and responsibilities should be fulfilled and by whom. Yet there were numerous occasions (the cases of Sal, Tariq and Sam, in Chapter 2, and Mandy, Ghazella and Robby in this chapter) in all three Partnership areas where ambiguity and confusion occurred. In a further example, it was left to a recipient of services who, although deeply grateful to Connexions for the support it was giving to her adopted son, suggested a meeting of the different professional workers in order to prevent friction between them.

John had a turbulent history from a very early age, having been abused, abandoned and taken into care at the age of one year. He was adopted but, especially in his teens, he had difficulties and conflicts at home and at school. He had truanted from school during the 16-plus examination period and left with no qualification, much to the exasperation of his adoptive parents. He joined the army but had been discharged after only a few days because of conflict with officers and other recruits. Violence and difficulties at home had led to him being referred to the Independent Living Team and housed in bed and breakfast accommodation. A Connexions PA who was a member of the team was told about his background, talked to him "for an hour-and-a-half", thought he was bright and deserved a second chance and arranged for him to start a college course on 'Uniformed Services'. With hindsight, his social worker was not sure this had been a good idea and regretted not sharing information about his history and background with the college, with John's consent. John's file was flagged indicating that care should be taken in dealing with him because of his temper:

> "I think that's my social work background ... he's had a lot of conflict with his parents and that could hinder and prevent him from being in a learning environment. And I think had we shared that with the college ... we might have been able to support him more."

His Connexions PA, although she had some doubts when she took him to see the college, thought he was someone she could really help:

> "'Cos I liked John straight away and I thought, 'Yes ... we'll get him sorted, that's all he needs. He just needs a chance to get in, once he got on to this course he'll be fine'.... I didn't look at the other sides ... there were a lot more underlying issues.

> "What I find as well with this job ... you're there to put them in, onto education and training. And I think sometimes they are not ready, they need a lot more time to be able to deal with all these other issues."

John was asked to leave the course because of conflict with tutors and other course members, found a place on another E2E course (including an anger management component) and allocated a participation trial Key Worker. It was at this point that his mother called a case conference that she felt was needed to clarify roles among the different workers involved.

There were signs, however, that the Partnerships were beginning to recognise the serious challenges they had in managing and supervising PAs. In all three study areas the management structures changed during the course of the research (see the Appendix). In Metborough, an additional tier of management was added, with the team of PAs employed by the local authority being broken into three different teams, each with their own manager responsible for day-to-day supervision. In Northern there was a growing recognition that the tasks and duties of the PA required much more support than the line management that had been in place within the careers companies. Support was felt to be necessary that was much more akin to close one-to-one supervision, and opportunities for all front-line staff to discuss aspects of their work with senior and experienced staff. In Midland Connexions and Metro Connexions supervision was being strengthened and prioritised. In all the study areas, team meetings – opportunities for PAs to meet together to discuss practical issues of cases they were dealing with and to share good practice – were becoming established.

Regular team meetings were seen by some PAs as one means of ensuring coordination, although it was recognised that these could be time-consuming. One PA in Midland Connexions for instance commented:

> "We don't have many formal meetings but we're going to start to because it's been raised a few times now, the three teams, you know, me and the CLASP [Children Looked After Support Panel] team and the PA need to meet more often."

At the time of the fieldwork in Metborough, careers company PAs and Youth Service PAs had separate team meetings, although there were plans to have joint 'away days' and 'recreationals' to encourage networking and working more closely together. In Northern, meetings of PAs were just beginning to take place in the spring of 2004 in an effort to share experience and good practice.

Confidentiality, information sharing and record keeping

One issue that remains difficult and unresolved within interagency working under Connexions concerns the recording and sharing of information. A general principle which all seemed to agree on was that information should not be kept or shared without the consent of the young person concerned. One PA commented:

> "I have in some cases bits of paper signed by young people saying I can share information. I haven't got that for all of them, but I've got their verbal agreement from the others, and every time we see somebody we remind them of the confidentiality policy."

Others in the same area were less clear:

> "I did ask them whether I could actually show my [project] colleagues what's on there. And I'm not really quite sure. I think again it's down to me checking with the young person. If they are happy with that and if I have their permission, each individual gives permission, then it was OK. If I don't then it wouldn't."

Information sharing was regarded as particularly problematic when this might include sensitive matters. The PA working with Ghazella's voluntary sector (at risk of prostitution) project, for instance, was very firm about the fact that none of her meetings or interventions at the project should be recorded on the Connexions computer system. There was an agreement in place between her manager and the project to that effect. The Sure Start Plus worker also had clients who were supported by the same project, but she was a little more ambivalent about such tightly interpreted restrictions:

> "We don't get any information from [the project].… I think it's because of the nature of the organisation, because they're dealing with a lot of child protection and vulnerable young girls, you know.… What the project will do,

they'll ring me up and ask me to speak to A [another case]. They won't tell me why or, do you know what I mean, they sometimes do that. They will tell the young person everything but they don't tell you anything really."

This worker did not have access to the Connexions database and there were no plans for this to happen in the future. However, because of strong *informal* links, information could be shared without paperwork changing hands and without anyone having to log on to the system, as she explained:

"Yeah, I'll ring individual PAs and talk to them about young people and do it that way, but I don't know about a higher level."

Sometimes formal protocols about joint working were in place, although these seem better developed and more widespread in Midland Connexions, the longer established the Partnership. Even here, on occasions, not all relevant agencies had yet been included.

"There was a protocol that was set up between social services, Connexions and the LSC, that [National Children's Charity] weren't involved in at all ... so that was sort of at very high level, and [the charity], for whatever reason, I don't really know why, but they weren't involved in it."

There was a general consensus that suggested that, if the technology permitted, professionals should share information on a 'need to know' basis. But it was less clear what that meant and when information might be deemed relevant and when it would not. Often, it may only come to light that workers 'needed to know' something when it is too late and the damage caused by not knowing has already been done. In Midland Connexions, Connexions staff working with offenders and ex-offenders were given access to information on YOT files. In Northern at the time of the research, no such agreement was in place and there was no expectation of information sharing with the YOT. Yet, as is shown in the case of Tariq (in Chapter 2), such sharing might have enabled a more complete assessment and intervention to be made. In Metborough, PAs in both the YOT and the Leaving Care Team had

access to the same information as case workers and social workers, but only because they were part of the multidisciplinary team. This did not apply to Connexions colleagues working elsewhere. This suggested that, outside of formal protocols or agreements, it was easier to share information with workers who were more obviously working within the agency.

In Midland Connexions, there was evidence about how complete openness in sharing information could disadvantage a young person. In some cases, revealing an on-going problem around drug use could have implications for being allocated housing, as one PA reported:

"I did take a young person to one of the housing places, he had an interview and I told him to be open and honest, and it was about that he smoked cannabis but he wouldn't do it on the premises. And, you know, he was getting some help from a counsellor about that. And as soon as he said that they said 'No'.... So then he went away thinking, 'Well if that's the reason, I'm not going to tell ... I'm not going to tell them'."

Being honest about previous criminal convictions was another issue, as the same PA explained:

"If you're working with a young person, looking at employment, then they never really want to tell the employer that they've got offences. So it's working with them and trying to make them understand why it is best to do that. But it's still their choice. But when we're working with providers, you know, we have a responsibility that we have to inform them about a young person's offences. As in with housing associations, we've got information protocols with two of the housing agencies, so we would just attach their list of offences."

Many PAs remained wary about the benefits of everything being recorded on the Connexions database system (CCIS) and about the time and value of continually trying to keep records up to date:

"Communication is so time-consuming and takes such a lot of energy, and the time just goes by between people being off or on training or getting back to you and [pause] but the system, I think, is fraught with difficulties."

Others reported that even sharing written reports with colleagues was still contentious:

"It's mainly for Personal Advisers but then again some admin staff need to be able to know those details, so some people are extremely guarded, even within the company, of sharing it with other people in the company, what they put on that system."

Others were unconvinced that the information was always illuminating or reliable, and many PAs in all three areas complained that the system was time-consuming and sometimes led to wrong impressions being formed. As with all databases, CCIS could only be as good as the data entered on it:

"You'll get completely the wrong view of somebody. Like I got told I couldn't do a home visit because there was an incident with an axe, and the way it was worded I was led to believe the young person was the one that had the axe. As it turns out the young person was chased down the road by very big guys with axes ... and he's now living somewhere else where it's quite safe. And I think he would have benefited from me visiting him at home.

"So that someone again hasn't updated the information they've put on. And that's another problem."

Issues around information sharing have become increasingly important in the light of developments following the Green Paper *Every child matters* (DfES, 2004a) . These will be reviewed in the next chapter.

Summary

This chapter has reviewed a number of different aspects of interagency working undertaken within Connexions Partnerships. It has identified a number of different levels of operation in which the networks are designed and operated. The chapter has also examined how front-line staff try to establish good working relationships with young people and the ways in which the different facets of interagency networking impacts on this. At its best, well-established networks allow for positive sharing of information at the point of referral and allow PAs to move quickly from the identification of needs to the means through which these needs can be met. Again, well-established and well-managed interagency networks make it easier to broker in services, and, where necessary, act as advocates for young people. The case studies included in this research have had at their core young people who represent the apex of the triangle of need; they were the most severe, complex, and most likely to require specialist and multiagency support. What is clear both from the illustrative case studies presented in Chapter 2 and the evidence presented in this chapter, is that there are still many instances where interagency networks are not strong, well-established or well-managed. The final chapter examines what is required for these issues to be addressed more effectively in the future.

4

Building better Connexions

The Connexions Strategy is one of the major service reforms to have been introduced by the Labour government in its attempt to bring more coherence to youth policy and to address problems of social exclusion. In Chapter 1 we reviewed the background to its introduction, some of the main principles and building blocks on which it is based, together with the challenges to be faced in interagency working. We also outlined how the Connexions Strategy was being implemented in the three Partnership areas covered by the research and how they had approached the challenges of establishing interagency working. There were marked differences experienced in the three research sites and these had influenced both the speed of partnership development and the contexts within which PAs worked. Chapter 2 outlined three case studies of young people with whom the Connexions Service was working in the three study areas as a precursor to a discussion of the issues being faced in interagency work. This latter was the focus of Chapter 3. In this final chapter we summarise some of the main findings of the research (F1-F9) in the first part of the chapter, together with recommendations for action (R1-R12) that follow from these findings. We then review the impact of the different models of partnership on interagency working and factors that are of equal importance. Finally, we review the policy debates that are ongoing at the time of writing. These suggest a likely re-configuration of Connexions in the near future in order to meet new arrangements being proposed for services for children and young people. Associated with this review and in line with the research findings, we add recommendations (R13-20) for the effective integration of Connexions into these service arrangements.

Summary of the main findings from the research

The research set out to examine interagency work under Connexions, to find examples of good practice and barriers to interagency working, and to examine whether different models of partnership development had an impact on the delivery of services to young people. Chapters 2 and 3 contained several examples of Connexions PAs playing a vital role in promoting the well-being of young people, often in partnership with other professional workers. It included examples where services were not as well coordinated as they might have been, where opportunities for information sharing were absent or severely limited. In some cases, Connexions PAs were only marginally involved and covered situations where vulnerable young people were not being well-supported by other professional workers with whom they were in contact. Yet even where interagency relationships were not working well, many of the young people themselves (and in one case a parent) went out of their way to express their appreciation of the help and support they had been given. Below we summarise some of the findings in more detail in order to highlight areas where lessons can be learned and improvements may be made.

Role definitions

F1: The term 'Personal Adviser' covered a multitude of very different roles and, because of this, was potentially confusing to some partners.

F2: One specific tension in the type of roles played by PAs was between those whose work was generic and related to an holistic assessment of the needs and those whose role was either entirely constrained within, or primarily directed by, a focus on careers education and guidance. Lack of clarity, particularly in schools, had bred suspicion that the Connexions Service was merely a re-badging of careers companies. It also left partners unclear about the authority of Connexions PAs.

Some school-based PAs had very large caseloads and, as such, were doing work which was closely aligned to the careers education and guidance role fulfilled prior to the arrival of Connexions. Some head teachers (such as the head of a special needs school in Nortown, quoted in Chapter 3) were bitterly disappointed and disillusioned that little had changed in the service they were offered. Confusion about, or resistance to, the role of PA, especially in schools, had also hindered effective interagency working (as in the case of Sam and Sal in Chapter 2). PAs with much smaller caseloads were, however, able to be very flexible and adaptable in responding to young people's needs, sometimes acting as a combination of personal secretary and parent as much as a careers adviser, broker and advocate.

In the final interview with the Chief Executive Officer in Metro Connexions, we were told that, latterly, the Partnership had worked very hard to blur the distinction between Careers PAs and Connexions PAs. We were told that great efforts had been made to create a unitary service in which the PA (no matter under which contract they were employed) was required to be flexible and play whatever role was needed. This raises questions about the extent to which PAs with very high caseloads can also find the time to undertake complex assessments and offer intensive support.

R1. Greater clarity should be provider for PAs about the specific role(s) they are expected to play, relating to their particular deployment.
R2. Better systems of referral should be developed between PAs with large caseloads and those able to offer intensive support.

R3. Greater clarity should be provided for agencies about the roles PAs working with them will play. This should also be accompanied with information about any opportunities the PA has to broker in support from other workers who can offer specialist or intensive support. Where appropriate, consideration should also be given to the range of job titles that might better aid understanding, for example, PA (Key Worker), PA (Careers Adviser).

Referrals

How cases were referred to Connexions PAs was reviewed in Chapter 3. Our major finding here is summarised below.

F3. Patterns of referral to PAs are very variable. Informal referral is often accompanied by insufficient background information. However, flexibility in the ways in which referrals were received sometimes helped to strengthen partnerships.

In Midland Connexions more formal referral often depended on agreements about patterns of joint working and information sharing (see below). In the other two areas informal referrals, sometimes based on a single telephone call, were more common and PAs started with little background information and were sometimes propelled into taking action before a proper assessment of need had been made (as in the case of John in Chapter 3). This was most apparent in Northern where Key Workers often had to begin work on the basis of a short telephone call.

R4. Across all agencies, wider commitment to accompanying referrals with full information is needed.

Coordination of roles

The main focus of this report is on interagency work where it is highly likely that more than one worker will be involved in trying to help a young person.

F4. Where a young person had more than one professional worker working with them, formal attempts to coordinate roles through case conferences were infrequently reported.

Chapter 3 summarised numerous cases where a number of different professional workers were all trying to help the same young person. Sometimes, and especially in Midland Connexions, there was evidence of good coordination of effort (as in the case of an asylum seeker in Midland Connexions reported in Chapter 3). In the other two areas, meetings between workers, face-to-face or over the telephone, were seldom found. This ran the risk of duplication of effort (as in the case of Sam in Chapter 2), placements misjudged, or needs not being met (as in the case of John and Ghazella in Chapter 3). Although team meetings of PAs were beginning to be organised in all three areas, case conferences were not commonplace. Often team meetings were restricted to those employed by specific contract holders rather than across the whole network of PAs. In the final interview with the Chief Executive Officer of Metro Connexions, however, we were told that these separate meetings had been replaced by meetings of all PAs across the borough.

R5. There is a need for PAs to be more aware of the value of systematic and regular communication between all workers working with the same client and the importance of formal case conferences, to share information, and to agree roles and actions.

Information sharing

One crucially important element supporting interagency work concerns the sharing of information.

F5. Information sharing between Connexions PAs and others was most likely when the PA was located within a multiagency team. Even when this PA had access to information it was often highly unlikely that information would be shared across the Connexions Service more generally or with other PAs outside of this team.

The research also indicated that some PAs were anxious about too much credence being given to electronic records which may be inaccurate, misleading or could quickly become out of date.

F6. There was some recognition by PAs that information, together with formal assessments, can be partial, incomplete or misleading. The fact of it being electronically stored and widely available to specific networks of professionals did not reduce its fallibility.

One of the risks of sharing information lay in the potential for forfeiting the need for Connexions to complete a further (possibly different and/or more complete) assessment. The research draws attention to the crucial importance of formal agreements and protocols for joint working in facilitating interagency work.

F7. Protocols or agreements on information sharing were an important part of interagency work. Although (increasingly) they were in place in some partnerships, in two of the three covered by this research much remained to be done. This continued to be a major structural barrier to effective interagency work by front-line workers.

In the absence of formal agreements, PAs remain unclear about what they can, or should, do and this can result in incomplete identification of the needs of clients, and uninformed, or misjudged, interventions.

R6. There is a need for more systematic information sharing between agencies and management, and supervision of PAs must support the value and importance of this. It is essential that information sharing becomes:
- *an integral part of the assessment process;*
- *continuous throughout any period of intensive support.*

This would be helped by clear protocols on information sharing between agencies.

Advocacy

Acting as an advocate for young people proved to be a most effective way in which PAs were supporting young people. Chapter 3 provided numerous examples of how this was being done to great effect.

F8. Advocacy on behalf of young people was clearly important as a means of preventing serious welfare harm, and ensuring that

young people received the benefits and services they needed and to which they were entitled. This role was sometimes played to good effect by some PAs, and young people welcomed their PAs as 'powerful friends'.

There is a need for greater clarity for all agencies with whom PAs work (and especially schools) about the legitimate responsibilities PAs have in terms of acting as advocates for young people.

R7. There is a need for clearer mechanisms through which managers can support the actions of PAs in acting as advocate for their clients and in challenging the routine practices of agencies where there is evidence of failures in service delivery.

Did the type of partnership model adopted make a difference to practice?

It is important to consider whether we have sufficiently robust evidence to offer an answer to the question as to whether the type of partnership makes a difference to the development and promotion of interagency working, and if so, the reasons for this. It is appropriate to review some of the reasons that make reaching firm conclusions on this question difficult. The three areas did indeed display the three different approaches to partnership described in the literature (OfSTED, 2002). But they differed in other ways. Midland Connexions had been operating longer than the other two Partnerships, although Metborough had piloted some aspects of Connexions the year before the full Partnership became operational. Midland Connexions covered only two local authorities. The others covered many more, which impacted on the complexity of their task. There were also differences of leadership style between the two areas that were not necessarily the result of the partnership model adopted, although the direct delivery model by its nature gave clear lines of influence in terms of staff management. Other factors contributing to different approaches to leadership could be explained by the personal characteristics, skills and beliefs of the post holders. All these aspects mediate the apparent influence of the structure. The research points to other factors that are also important in promoting and facilitating interagency work.

Joint working agreements

Agreements on joint working practices, protocols on aspects of joint working (including information sharing) are crucial in the effective promotion of partnership working. It is these that create the *structural* framework that both requires and supports agencies to work together. This can be fostered by Board-level activity, but, most importantly, must be put in place at a local authority level because it is here that many of the major agencies with which Connexions front-line staff have to work are located.

F9. The Connexions Strategy still faced structural problems in the promotion of effective interagency work, regardless of the type of partnership development model it has adopted. While managers of partner agencies may not have been wilfully preventing partnership working, in many circumstances the mechanisms which would promote it were not yet in place.

The case studies reviewed in Chapters 2 and 3 illustrated that, by and large, PAs were working to their maximum potential with complex cases in difficult circumstances. But it is also important to emphasise the need for further improvements in the *structural* framework in which Connexions work is carried out if the potential of the work done by PAs is to improve significantly. These conclusions directly contradict some of the findings of the Connexions Stakeholder Survey sponsored by the DfES. Summarising their findings the NAO contend:

> Where barriers to joint working have emerged, these have been local rather than national. The head quarters staff at the partner agencies and departments we consulted were broadly happy with their relationships with the Connexions Service and were clear about what Connexions wants to achieve. These partners did not feel that there were any *structural* reasons that would *prevent* Connexions partnerships working together with their staff at a local level. [They] agreed that *local relationships and personalities* were the crucial factors determining how quickly they were able to move to true partnership working. (NAO, 2004, p 4; emphasis added)

We regard these as potentially misleading. Our research demonstrates clearly that there were *structural* barriers to interagency working. Chapter 3 illustrated that mechanisms needed to be put in place at a structural level, with the agreement of partners, before they could affect or influence practice. The Connexions Strategy still faced *structural* problems in the promotion of effective interagency work, regardless of the type of partnership development model it has adopted.

R8. There is a need for clearer mechanisms through which managers can support the actions of PAs in acting as advocate for their clients and in challenging the routine practices of agencies where there is evidence of failures in service delivery.

Perhaps understandably, the longest established partnership, Midland Connexions, appeared to have developed and implemented more agreements and protocols than was the case in Metborough and Nortown. Senior managers in Midland Connexions had been proactive in engaging in both formal and informal negotiation with agencies to reassure and reconfirm the involvement of partner agencies in the Connexions Strategy. They saw this as a fundamental part of their job.

In Metborough, at the time of our research, the structure for interagency work was much less developed. Some stakeholders interviewed said they were reluctant to sign up to Connexions, partly because of continued confusion about the relationship between Careers, the Connexions Service and the Connexions Strategy. Some positive interagency work was occurring, but this depended on the individual skills of the PA rather than the planned structural environment in which they worked. Furthermore, in some circumstances the practices of key partners (such as the social services department) contributed to the barriers to learning being faced by young people. This was something that the Connexions PAs could not resolve alone.

The structural framework for interagency working in Nortown was also poorly developed. Again, some positive interagency work was taking place, but often despite, rather than because of, the partnership frameworks developed by Connexions itself. Much depended on either interagency working developed

elsewhere or the skills of the individual PA, many of whom were working within a structure and context that was often limiting rather than facilitating interagency work. It is notable that some effective interagency work, including taking on the role of advocate, was being carried out by professional workers other than Connexions PAs.

R9. The management and supervision of Connexions PAs needs to be strengthened. Action by managers is needed on several fronts:
- **the negotiation of agreements on joint working with partner agencies at a local level;**
- **supporting PAs in their role as advocate for the young person and ensuring that they fulfil this role, even in situations in which there is resistance from partner agencies; and**
- **ensuring compliance of partner agencies in the proper fulfilment of the responsibilities.**

In support of the above:

R10. There is need for better communication between management and PAs about precisely what protocols and agreements on joint working are in place.

Training

The 2004 NAO report on Connexions contains some evidence that Partnerships following the 'direct delivery model' have been quicker in moving towards the completion of the training of PAs than subcontracting partnerships (NAO, 2004). A chart in the report does indeed show Midland Connexions significantly ahead of both Northern and Metro Connexions. Interviews with senior managers and Board members in Midland Connexions confirmed that they placed a high value and priority on training, despite recognising the costs to the Partnership in terms of staff time spent in not performing front-line tasks (see the Appendix). The direct delivery model does also give manages more direct control over how to organise staff time. Subcontracting partnerships must rely on managers of agencies holding the contracts complying with training demands. Our research indicates that contracting agencies were indeed making efforts to ensure that PAs completed professional diploma training.

R11. There is a continued need for training of:
- *PAs to hone the variety of skills they must use;*
- *mid-level managers in supervising and supporting PAs, particularly with reference to trouble-shooting the structural problems surrounding interagency work;*
- *co-workers in other agencies, in respect of the responsibilities of Connexions PAs and the changing structure of services.*

Communicating the vision

In all three partnership areas many attempts were made by Connexions staff to meet with potential partners to explain what the Connexions Strategy was and what the implications of it were for other organisations and agencies. The occasions varied from face-to-face meetings of senior staff to multimedia presentations at large gatherings in school halls, hotels and football stadia. Midland Connexions placed considerable emphasis on communicating the vision of Connexions to other partners, encouraging cultural change in working practices and encouraging senior managers to engage in partnership building to foster joint projects. They had also done so in a way that was beginning to break down some of the barriers between the two local authority areas. Starting initially with the activities of the chief executive, transmitting the vision of Connexions increasingly had become the duty of all managers.

Not all such missionary work had positive outcomes. The head teacher of a special needs school in Nortown (referred to in Chapter 3) was particularly critical, seeing staged events as expensive, unnecessary and time-consuming when he would have preferred to have seen the money spent on front-line services. Another head teacher in Metborough, although acknowledging that Connexions had made a big impact on the most vulnerable in the Borough, thought it was 'the universal service' that was losing out (see the Appendix).

R12. As Connexions enters a new period in which it has to operate alongside other agencies charged with the coordination of services for children and young people, there remains a need for clear communication to partner agencies about the Connexions Strategy and the roles and responsibilities of the Connexions Service in delivering this will be vital (see recommendations R13-R20 below).

The changing policy contexts for the Connexions Strategy

Chapter 1 outlined the policy context that gave rise to the Connexions Strategy, focusing especially on the drive to prevent the social exclusion of vulnerable young people and to offer positive routes back to those who experienced it. The case studies outlined in Chapters 2 and 3 illustrate the processes and the help Connexions is offering to a variety of different vulnerable groups of young people. Towards the end of our fieldwork we were told that, within the upper echelons of the senior Civil Service and in government, few talked about the 'Connexions Strategy' any longer. The wider vision of joined-up and coordinated services for young people seemed to have dropped off the agenda, at least as far as Connexions was concerned. If this is the case, then we think it a retrograde step, although it was always ambitious for the Connexions Service alone to be charged with the delivery of the strategy. Perhaps a more likely situation is that the challenges faced by the strategy are now recognised to have a much wider relevance to services for children and young people across all age groups, and that the mechanisms through which these will be faced require different structures and processes than the Connexions Partnerships alone can provide.

The policy context for Connexions changed considerably during the lifetime of this research, and the emergence of a new set of initiatives offers a possibility that the Connexions Strategy can be reshaped and revitalised. Three main initiatives suggest this.

Children and Young People Strategic Partnerships (CYPSPs)

The first concerns the development within local authorities of Children and Young People's Strategic Partnerships (CYPSPs). These were at various stages of development in each of our research sites. Because this included children as well as young people, more services were involved than was covered by Connexions Partnerships, although Connexions (as a major commissioner of services) was certainly included.

The similarities between CYPSPs and the initial prospectus for the Connexions Strategy lie in the range of anticipated partners, such as schools, health, social services, police and YOTs. The major difference, however, lies not so much in the age range covered or the number of services involved (Sure Start, Early Years Partnerships, Children's Fund and so on), but the fact that the CYPSPs were conducted by, and for, single-tier local authorities. This is important for a number of reasons. First, local authorities have the authority to persuade, and if necessary to instruct, their constituent departments and managers to become involved. Those from other agencies within CYPSPs, such as health, youth justice and the voluntary sector, are quasi-autonomous. But these often have a long-established relationship with the local authority and a history of working together. This is in contrast to subregional Connexions Partnerships where, as we have already noted, partners could not compel their constituencies to cooperate. Within some Connexions Partnerships some partners offered resistance and, on occasions, downright hostility to the Partnership. There is, therefore, a real possibility that the grand ambitions for the initial Connexions Strategy may dissolve in the face of an alternative and more mandatory partnership arrangement being developed. CYPSPs do not set out deliberately to replace or undermine the Connexions Strategy. But CYPSPs are based across structures where frequently there are common local identities, loyalties, a history of partnership, and most importantly, are promoted by those with authority, access to resources and teeth.

The *Every child matters* policy agenda

The second set of initiatives seem to reinforce such developments. The Green Paper *Every child matters* produced in the wake of an inquiry into the death of Victoria Climbié promised consultation on better systems of information sharing and a structural reconfiguration of responsibilities and services for children and young people (Chief Secretary to the Treasury, 2003). These developments have some resonance, both with the findings of our research and with the development within local authorities of CYPSPs as outlined above. A number of the suggested reforms deserve comment.

The first reform concerns the proposal for the creation of Children's Trusts. These are designed to play a central coordinating role within a single-tier local authority in commissioning services for children and young people. All local authorities will be required to appoint a Director of Children's Services, accountable for education and social services and responsible for overseeing services commissioned from elsewhere. This Director will be supported by an elected council member who would be designated as the lead council member for children. Children's Trusts will be responsible for the full range of outcomes concerning children and young people's welfare, planning and commissioning services supported by pooled budgets.

The range of institutions covered by Children's Trusts include minimally: all the educational functions of the LEA (including schools, educational welfare, educational psychology, special educational needs, child care and early years provision and youth services); children's social services (including assessment, fostering, residential care and adoption, child protection and services for care leavers); and community and acute health services (including community paediatrics, Drug Action Teams [DATs], teenage pregnancy, Child and Adolescent Mental Health Services [CAMHs], health visiting and speech therapy). In addition to this range, the Green Paper encourages Children's Trusts to consider covering the coordination of YOTs and the Connexions Service. This suggests that the planning of services would be clearly in the hands of the Children's Trusts. The Green Paper suggests that the Children's Trusts could also act as the LMC for Connexions, that the total Connexions resource available to the authority should be clearly identified, and that, although the final say concerning these lay with Connexions Chief Executive Officers, Connexions business plans should be signed off by Children's Trusts before ministers are asked to agree them. This suggests that, particularly in areas where there were continuing disputes, the emergence of Children's Trusts would signal a rebalancing of power away from subregional partnerships and back towards single-tier local authorities. Following the consultation period, this became even clearer as the government announced its *Next steps* (DfES, 2004a):

> ... strengthening the business planning guidance to ensure that Connexions Partnerships increasing delegate funding and planning decisions down to the Local Management Committee.

It also announced that pilots would take place through which PAs would have not only brokerage and advocate roles, but purchasing powers with discretionary budgets to purchase services for young people.

Another important concern relates to the development of electronic records and proposals for information sharing between agencies. This has become know as IRS as it is intended that it will cover identification, referral and support. A precursor of this, IRT (identification, referral and tracking) has been piloted by 15 local authorities since autumn 2002 and an interim report on progress was published in 2004 (Cleaver et al, 2004). Many of these pilots were based on the use of the Common Assessment Framework published by the Department of Health, DfES and Home Office in 2000, rather than either ASSET or APIR. However, the research on the IRT pilots has some similarities with the findings of our research: that practitioners were uncertain about what information they could legally share; the lack of compatibility of computer systems between agencies; variability in the competence of front-line staff; but little reluctance on the part of young people for information to be shared (indeed some surprise where it was not). Clearly decisions need to be made as soon as possible about a framework for information sharing and how the major systems including those used by YOTs and Connexions will fit into these. The current proposals are for an 'information hub'

with basic data for all children and young people (with a unique identification number) also being linked to a 'flag' system indicating if the person is known to other agencies and giving the contact details of the worker(s) involved.

The proposed improvements to information systems are also closely linked with identification and allocation of the 'lead professional'. Connexions spent a great deal of effort providing options for the coordination of different workers and in determining who should play the lead role (Connexions, 2002a-e). Yet as our research has indicated, there are still examples of workers not being coordinated, and consequently instances of both duplication of effort, and young people falling through the gaps, and information not being shared. The Green Paper argues for the co-location of multidisciplinary teams around places where young people spend their time and the importance of embedding targeted services within universal, non-stigmatising, service settings. Connexions One-Stop-Shops offer an opportunity to do this, but our research has indicated some difficulties in the process. Locating PAs in other agencies opened the door to information sharing for the PAs so located, but often did not provide more general access for all relevant PAs across the Partnership.

The Green Paper also calls for discussion about radical proposals for workforce reform. One of the key strategic aims is that those working with children and young people should be enabled to work across professional boundaries, are trained to do their own job well, but also understand how it fits in with the work of others. Connexions has its own training programmes: a level 3 diploma course for PAs and an 'Understanding Connexions' course for other workers. However, as more and more PAs have completed their diploma training, the continuation of the programme itself is in doubt. In addition to taking the diploma course, PAs are also expected to have their own professional qualifications in areas such as youth work or careers educational guidance. The Green Paper announced a new Children's Workforce Unit within the DfES to support professional training and to help build bridges between different qualifications and enhance promotion prospects. But, as the Paper recognises, "As joint working becomes the norm, clarity about roles and responsibilities will become all the more important".

The development of the 'youth offer'

A third set of policy initiatives emerged in the summer of 2004 with the publication of a five-year plan by the DfES (DfES, 2004b). Chapter Six of the Plan deals with 14-19 education training but it is most concerned with the post-compulsory education years. International comparisons show the UK as low on the league table for participation among 17-year-olds and this is argued to be the precursor to low adult skills. The proposed solution is a mixture of more choice, higher standards, a better mix of academic and vocational courses and good sources of advice, guidance and support. There are proposals too about a new integrated 'youth offer' related not only to post-16 courses but more positive "exciting and enjoyable activities to do in and out of school or college", "chances to get involved", and places to go in the communities in which young people live (DfES, 2004b). There is, of course, also mention of groups known to be vulnerable and seriously disadvantaged. It is difficult *not* to recognise within this portfolio the prospectus for the 1999 Connexions Strategy. Yet there are some differences of emphasis. The use of the term 'offer' is close to both the 'youth pledge' developed for the Youth Service (DfES, 2002) and to 'entitlements' and 'rights' – terms used in Wales when they chose not to go down the Connexions route but to develop their own strategy for children and young people (WAG, 2002, 2004). This provides another opportunity to build a closer alliance between Connexions work and the wider and more voluntaristic leisure, personal and social developmental activities associated with youth work.

Another key consideration is how the 'youth offer' will be delivered. The plan recognises that too much support for young people is currently 'fragmented'; worthwhile, but with overlapping aims and too many funding streams. It contends that better coordination of effort is required. Again, the lead bodies proposed to develop this are not Connexions Partnerships but Children's Trusts, although the plan does emphasise that these should "build on the principles and success of multidisciplinary and collaborative working introduced by Connexions" (DfES, 2004b). A

further Green Paper on Young People is promised for the autumn of 2004. Given that the five-year plan was announced simultaneously with the 2004 Comprehensive Spending Review, whatever rearrangements are to be proposed must be found within an overall budget that already has been set. Three main funding priorities now compete within the general parameters of Connexions work: mainstream careers education and guidance; targeted support for vulnerable groups; and activities programmes for young people including school and non-school-based sports and personal development.

Rebuilding better Connexions

The combination of the policy initiatives reviewed in this chapter calls into question whether subregional Connexions Partnerships may soon be eclipsed by Children's Trusts and how the Connexions Service will be reconfigured once Children's Trusts have been developed. To aid this latter process and to help promote better interagency work in future years we offer the following recommendations:

R13. Guidance is needed from government on the links between the Connexions Strategy, the Connexions Service and the roles and responsibilities of Children's Trusts.

R14. Discussions between Connexions and the statutory and voluntary youth services would be useful to explore how their services could be more closely integrated under the 'youth offer'. Some coordination with these with the activity programmes funded by the Youth Justice Board and local YOTs would also be useful.

R15. Direction must come from government about the extent to which pooling of budgets within Children's Trusts will be mandatory or discretionary.

R16. Exemplars from government would be helpful on protocols for information sharing and guidance on the circumstances in which 'need to know' criteria are triggered.

R17. It would be wise for early negotiations to begin between Connexions Partnerships, Children and Young People Strategic Partnerships and Children's Trusts on the allocation of roles and responsibilities. Experience from the development of Connexions suggests this might best take the form of a series of bi-lateral meetings to allay anxieties and fears.

R18. It would be helpful to have an open review between Connexions senior management and Children's Trusts about how decisions about 'lead professionals' will be reached and reviewed and what this means for the role and responsibilities of Connexions PAs.

R19. There remains a need for the development of mechanisms through which advocacy for young people can be supported and disputes between agencies can be resolved.

R20. There is need for discussion about what range of services and supports needs to be organised at a subregional level and what might best be delegated to local authorities and Children's Trusts. This may also have implications for the size of the Connexions Partnership top-slice of the funding they receive and the size of the subregional team.

This research has revealed mixed fortunes for Connexions Partnerships in their first years of operation. There is evidence that the Partnerships are well on their way to meeting their key target of reducing the numbers of young people who are NEET (NAO, 2004). At their best, Connexions PAs have provided much-needed support for young people, have brokered opportunities for them and have acted as powerful advocates on their behalf. Yet in none of the three Partnerships has the work of PAs in this regard been straightforward. The arrival of Children's Trusts and the proposals for the transformation of the professions working with children and young people offer new opportunities for the bold ambitions of the Connexions Strategy to be given a fresh lease of life.

References

Atkinson, M., Wilkin, A., Stott, A., Doherty, P. and Kinder, K. (2002) *Multi-agency working: A detailed study*, Slough: National Federation for Educational Research.

Bentley, T. and Gurumurthy, R. (1999) *Destination unknown: Engaging with the problems of marginalised youth*, London: DEMOS.

Britton, L., Chatrik, B., Coles, B., Craig, G., Hylton, C. and Mumtaz, S. (2002) *Missing Connexions?: The career dynamics and welfare needs of 16-17 year olds*, Bristol/York: The Policy Press/Joseph Rowntree Foundation.

Chief Secretary to the Treasury (2003) *Every child matters*, Government Green Paper, Cm 5960, London: DfES.

Cleaver, H., Barnes, J., Bliss, D. and Cleaver, D. (2004) *Developing identification, referral and tracking systems: An evaluation of the processes undertaken by trailblazer authorities: Interim report*, DfES Research Report No 521, London: University of London.

Coles, B. (2000) *Joined-up youth research, policy and practice: The new agenda for change?*, Leicester: Youth Work Press/Barnardo's.

Coles, B. (2004) 'Better connections? Welfare services for young people', in J. Roche, S. Tucker, R. Thomson and R. Flynn (eds) *Youth in society* (2nd edn), London: Sage Publications.

Coles, B., Hutton, S., Bradshaw, J.R., Craig, G., Godfrey, C. and Johnson, J. (2002) *Literature review of the costs of being 'Not in Education, Employment or Training' at age 16-18*, Sheffield: DfES.

Connexions, (2001a) *Connexions Service business planning guidance October 2001*, London: DfES.

Connexions (2001b) *Connexions for all: Working to provide a service for all young people*, London: DfES.

Connexions and the Rough Sleepers Unit (2002a) *Working together: Connexions and youth homelessness agencies*, London: DfES.

Connexions and the Social Services Inspectorate (2002b) *Working together: Connexions and social services*, London: DfES.

Connexions and the Teenage Pregnancy Unit (2002c) *Working together: Connexions and teenage pregnancy*, London: DfES.

Connexions and the Youth Justice Board (2002d) *Working together: Connexions and youth justice services*, London: DfES.

Connexions (2002e) *The Connexions Service: A briefing guide for Drug Action Teams*, London: DfES.

Connexions (2002f) *Working together: Connexions with voluntary and community organisations*, London: DfES.

Connexions (2002g) *Youth support services for 13-19 year olds: A vision for 2006: How Connexions will deliver this*, Sheffield: Connexions Service National Unit.

Connexions (2003a) *Working together: Connexions supporting young asylum seekers and refugees*, London: DfES.

Connexions (2003b) *Understanding Connexions: Participants' file*, Sheffield: Connexions.

Connexions (2004) *Diploma for Connexions personal advisers: Module 4 Handbook*, Sheffield: Connexions Service.

CRG Research (2002) *An investigation into the use of the Connexions Assessment, Planning, Implementation and Review (APIR) framework*, Research Report RR372, London: DfES.

DfEE (Department for Education and Employment) (1999) *Learning to succeed: A new framework for post-16 learning*, Cm 4392, London: The Stationery Office.

DfEE (2000) *Connexions: The best start in life for every young person*, Nottingham: DfEE.

DfES (Department for Education and Skills) (2002) *Transforming youth work: Resourcing excellent youth services*, London: DfES.

DfES (2004a) *Every child matters: Next steps*, London: DfES.

DfES (2004b) *Department for Education and Skills: Five year strategy for children and learners. Putting people at the heart of public services*, London: The Stationery Office.

Godfrey, C., Hutton, S., Bradshaw, J., Coles, B., Craig, G. and Johnson, J. (2002) *Estimating the cost of being 'Not in Education, Employment or Training' aged 16-18*, Research Report RR346, London: DfES.

NAO (National Audit Office) (2004) *Connexions Service: Advice and guidance for all young people*, Report by the Comptroller and Auditor General, HC 484, 2003-04, 31 March, London: The Stationery Office.

OECD (Organisation for Economic Co-operation and Development) (2003) *OECD Review of Careers Guidance Policies: United Kingdom, Country Note* (www.oecd.org/LongAbstract/ 0,2546,en_2649_34511_4522837_70432_119663_1_1,00.html).

OfSTED (2002) *Connexions Partnerships: The first year 2001-2002*, HM1521, London: OfSTED.

Pierce, N. and Hillman, J. (1998) *Wasted youth: Raising achievement and tackling social exclusion*, London: Institute for Public Policy Research.

Skelcher, C., Mathur, N. and Smith, M. (2004) *Effective partnership and good governance: Conformance or performance*, ESRC Research Summary (Executive summary and full report available online).

SEU (Social Exclusion Unit) (1998) *Truancy and exclusion*, Cm 3957, London: The Stationery Office.

SEU (1999) *Bridging the gap: New opportunities for 16-18 year olds not in education, employment or training*, Cm 4405, London: The Stationery Office.

WAG (Welsh Assembly Government) (2002) *Framework for partnership*, Cardiff: WAG.

WAG (2004) *Children and young people: Rights to action*, Cardiff: WAG.

Williamson, H. (1997) 'Status Zero youth and the "underclass"', in R. MacDonald (ed) *Youth, the 'underclass' and social exclusion*, London: Routledge.

Appendix:
The (trans)formation of the three Partnerships

This Appendix describes in more detail than was possible in Chapter 1 the three Partnership areas in which the research took place. It describes the development of the three Partnerships, and the deployment and management of front-line workers together with the challenges these presented to Connexions. We draw on official documents, Connexions business plans, reports and, where possible, the observation of meetings. Based on the interviews with key stakeholders, it also describes some of the ways used to implement the Connexions Strategy and factors that supported or hindered this being achieved effectively.

The names of the three Partnerships, and those of all those interviewed during the course of the research are referred to by pseudonyms only. As outlined in Chapter 1, Midlands Connexions was one of the early pilots and started operating in spring 2001. Metro Connexions had piloted some aspects of Connexions in separate boroughs in 2001-02, but did not start as a fully-fledged Partnership until the summer of 2002. Northern Connexions started in the autumn of 2002. Within Metro Connexions and Northern we examined the planning and implementation of services in only one of the local authority areas covered by the Partnership. In Metro Connexions the borough is referred to as Metborough, and the Metropolitan District which is the focus of attention within Northern we identify as Nortown.

Midland Connexions

Midland Connexions was the smallest of the three Partnership areas, covering just over 81,000 young people aged 13-19 from just two local authority areas. The area covered by the Partnership included one medium-sized city and a shire county, with a number of small- to medium-sized market towns. Approximately 60% of young people were located in the city. According to a needs analysis conducted in 2003, the young people who were not in education, employment or training (NEET), had complex problems and needed one-to-one caseload support represented around 10%; those in need of additional support over and above the 'universal service' numbered around 37%; and those for whom there was a universal entitlement only were around 53% of the age cohorts. More specific target groups identified in the business plan included 16- to 19-year-old mothers, 13- to 18-year-olds with substance misuse problems, 19-year-old care leavers, 13- to 18-year-olds supervised by YOTs, and 16- to 19-year-olds with learning difficulties and disabilities.

Midland Connexions

Midland Connexions Partnership was part of an economic and regeneration company, limited by guarantee, which directly employed most of the staff working for Connexions. As a direct deliverer of services, approximately 78% of resources were committed to service delivery itself. Many, but by no means all, of the 316 staff were previously employed by two careers companies (which ceased trading in April 2002) covering the two local authorities. The company completed a European Foundation Quality Management (EFQM) self-assessment report, and was inspected by OfSTED in the autumn of 2002.

At strategic level, Midland Connexions Partnership Board was large compared with the others. At the outset, it was thought important for the Board to be as inclusive as possible in order to reassure potential partners of the importance of their role within the Partnership. Because the Board covered only two local authorities, originally there was a matching representation from each. When the Partnership became more established the frequency of meetings was reduced, and the Board met three times (termly) a year. In effect, the Partnership Board was described as having turned into a consultative forum supporting a more active Executive Group of 17 members and presided over by the Board Chair.

The two Local Management Committees (LMCs) of city and shire county were originally part of the organisational structure. These were not as large as the Partnership Board, and the frequency of meetings was also reduced over time. Changes were made in respect of chairing one of the committees. At one stage, plans were being made to incorporate the LMCs into a Management Group in order to prevent duplication of representation. The LMCs met twice a year and provided a forum for help in shaping the business plan and in reviewing progress. Initially these were chaired by the Chief Executive Officer of the two councils, but both were happy to delegate this role to others. As one senior officer put it:

> "It was important at the beginning. But there is no management in it. It is just a sounding board."

Liaison with the local authorities was carried out through informal meetings held around every two months between the Chief Executive Officer of Connexions, the local authority Chief Executive Officers, and the chief officers or deputies from education and social services. This was largely seen as an informal 'taking the temperature' meeting.

The Executive Group met more frequently than other groups (every six weeks), and there was speculation at the time of the research that it would evolve to meet less frequently in the future. In addition to these groups, there were:

> "... a number of management groups that either directly manage delivery or help coordinate support functions (HR, Finance, Quality). The subregional support managers group brings together

senior delivery and support function managers."

Services were based on those provided to 'clients who are in education' or those who are 'out of education'. Specialist staff did outreach work to specific groups, for example, drug users, young offenders and so on. Other staff were located within partner agencies, such as the voluntary sector and YOTs. There was a policy of siting both Connexions and partner agency staff in the same locations. There were 35 Connexions sites across the region, including three One-Stop-Shops and, in total, around 165 PAs.

One form of specialist provision was from a 'Learning Gateway Project', based at the Local Learning and Skills Council (LLSC). This continued after the Learning Gateway was replaced by Entry to Employment (E2E) in the summer of 2003. The project and the team were mainly concerned with supporting the 'front end' of Gateway (induction and one-to-one support) and also offering support to young people involved in life skills training – the 'back end' of Learning Gateway. The Learning Gateway Project started in December 2002 and had funding until December 2004. The project involved a small team of eight PAs. Six PAs were based with life skills providers. This was the first time that PAs had been based with training providers. The company also separately funded 'enhanced provision'. This included activities designed to improve confidence, social skills, and self-esteem, focusing on team-building activities at a sports centre, and special residential courses.

A further two PAs were based with the Teenage Pregnancy Strategy. One of these worked with young fathers, split between two sites where the teenage pregnancy rates were highest. The other was working with young mothers. All eight PAs were carrying out work described as 'firefighting' – emergency work attempting to deal with problems that might lead young people to disengage from learning and/or training.

The third element covered by the company was 'special services'. One of these was an independent psychological service that brought someone into the LLSC every three weeks to see young people whom providers thought needed such a service. Specialist support such as anger management courses were offered. The second service was the DDAT (Dyslexia, Dyspraxia,

Attention Deficit Disorder Treatment). The young people referred there may or may not have had a statement of special educational need (SEN). Training providers could refer young people to the centre if they thought they needed assessment and/or support. Other forms of specialist support were arranged by linking to YOTs and Drug Action Teams and other such services.

During the later stages of the research, links with the voluntary sector were planned and realised. Four pilot projects were funded and five PAs were allocated to provide support, liaison, and referrals, as well as to promote opportunities within the sector.

Issues in the development of partnership working in Midland Connexions

Senior managers of Midland Connexions Partnership told us that they had long recognised that building an effective team was not something which was achieved overnight. It needed a concerted effort at a number of different levels within the organisation and on a number of different fronts. They were also clear about the importance of political negotiation during the early stages of the development of the Partnership, ensuring that key stakeholders did not feel threatened by developments, recognised the advantages to be gained through cooperation, and were convinced that the effort involved was worthwhile. Most of this was achieved in individually tailored meetings rather than through discussion or debate within boardrooms. Indeed stakeholders had agreed that the more formal structures of decision making had become less necessary, and the frequency of such meetings had been reduced without resistance.

As well as this *horizontal* level of partnership formation, senior managers were also concerned that they had a responsibility to work *vertically* within the organisation and to communicate the company vision. With hindsight, it was said that this had not been as comprehensively accomplished in the early days of operation as it might have been. But senior managers came to address this on a number of fronts: selling the vision; investment in training; rewarding innovation and progress; and building self-belief, pride and morale.

Starting with the core of ex-careers advisers and especially those who welcomed change, the knowledge bases and skills of front-line workers were broadened to meet the requirements of Connexions PAs. The PAs interviewed expressed appreciation of the way in which senior managers had added to and developed their skills, largely through training. As a general principle, this was offered to PAs and partners at the same time, and although some partner agencies were notably enthusiastic (such as the voluntary sector where fewer courses in general existed), other partners remained harder to enjoin. Senior managers put effort into making training fit with the agendas of other agencies, and, in particular, ensuring that the timing of courses was appropriate to the needs of others.

More structural changes linked to redrawing the operational geographic boundaries of Connexions. Operations managers were drawn upwards in the hierarchy to function more strategically. As one explained:

> "There's a structural change, part of that was our trying to kick-start even further the cultural change that we've been going through. So we've now got people who were Midcity staff mixing with people who were Midtown staff from the new area and breaking down some of those city versus county working practices and traditions and systems."

This was part of a wider attempt to bring about greater receptivity to and understanding about Connexions across organisations. It was also geared towards making cultural change; in working practices, traditions, and systems within areas, and towards reducing the feeling of 'them' and 'us' which was frequently experienced when bringing together different organisations. Staff were now working across new areas and sites, in an attempt to increase both learning and reach:

> "So for instance I went to speak to the chief executive of X County Council [and then] his 27-strong management team, to tell them what Connexions does 'cos they've hardly heard of it unless they happen to be a parent.... So in that case it's telling the borough council what we do and how we link into the stuff that they're doing, how we'd like to link in and how we'd like to have some joint

initiatives, how we'd like to have some added value by working together. I suppose a stage on from that is going to the people who do know about us … which might be 'What are you doing stepping on our toes, doing the job?' … and explaining we're not really doing that, we're trying to do the same things and work[ing] together would be more effective and more efficient."

Connexions was seen in a positive light by those responsible for delivering services at local authority level, and the relationship was an evolving one throughout the course of the research. Connexions played a part in other organisations, for example, in a wider programme for young people aged 10 to 13, as well as a broader strategic multiagency plan which operated at Partnership level for vulnerable children and young people in one of its local authorities. As such, Connexions was seen as considerably influential within the context of wider partnerships.

Main issues with partner agencies were around levels of expectations, geographic and practice boundaries, and prioritisation. Expectations about Connexions varied according to organisations. Some were regarded as too high, some too low. Perceptions as to the encroachment on work territories already established prior to Connexions made practice boundaries sometimes difficult to cross, and geographic boundaries between partners did not always quite match. Conveying messages about the potential of Connexions throughout the vertical slice of organisations was problematic insofar as commitment from senior managers did not necessarily filter through to individual workers, who were often dealing with acute cases from wider population groups, for example, generic social workers dealing with potential child murderers. At an organisational level, some partners still remained hard to engage. This was usually seen to be for reasons concerned with their own major reorganisations (for example, health services), although individual workers (school nurses, for example) were more receptive to building links. Selling the vision and transmitting the Connexions message was seen as a continuing challenge, and more resources in terms of staff time were being committed to this. As the chief executive noted:

"I had a piece of feedback very early on from [names] and I got a load of feedback from all the staff about me. And they all said '[name of CEO], we think your energy, your vision, your aspirations, your passion, your desire, is absolutely fantastic and, you know, you just wow us, but for Christ's sake get realistic about what we can achieve in a month', you know. And I realised that I'd gone charging off and left all the middle managers and all the troops miles behind me, you know. So I had to go back and pick them all up and get them up off their knees and then move them on again, and that was really frustrating and, actually, it was really painful because my perception of how we were doing and what was happening and … their perception was completely different. So I had to change my behaviours, otherwise we'd have been totally fragmented … and now the … I can see them increasingly taking up the challenges and moving the challenges on, and all I have to do is just let them."

Pace, timing, and political sensitivities each played a part in achieving a unified approach. The important point was that Midland Connexions staff showed keen awareness of what needed to be considered in achieving a shared vision, and this was a major contributor to successful negotiations.

Metro Connexions and Metborough

Metro Connexions covered a number of boroughs across a section of a very large city containing over 100,000 young people aged 13 to 19 years. The boroughs varied considerably in their demographic composition, the problems they faced, their political complexion and their reputation for the delivery of services. One very distinctive feature of Metborough involved the mobility of its inhabitants and the sharp contrasts of wealth and poverty in close proximity. There were, for instance, 11 independent schools, more than the number of secondary and special schools combined.

Establishing the size of the Connexions (13-19) cohort for Metborough was not an easy business. The careers company estimated it to be around

6,000, whereas Census data indicates there just over ten and a half thousand 13- to 19-year-olds. This suggested a much higher number of residents in the school-based Connexions cohort, although they may, of course, have been in independent schools or educated outside the borough. Only around half of the pupils in Metborough schools were resident in the borough and many of those resident were in education elsewhere, some in areas served by Connexions Services other than Metro Connexions.

Metborough was ethnically mixed with over a hundred different languages spoken in its schools and more than a thousand refugees in its secondary schools (around 12% of the school population). The second largest group was 'Black African', the third 'Indian' and the largest group of all was classified as 'Other' according to the statistics in the business plan. Metborough schools have high rates of mobility, non-attendance and permanent exclusions. Non-attendance was a particular problem in Metborough which, at 3.1%, was the highest rate across the Partnership. Black children, especially boys, were over-represented on the child protection register, and rates of mental illness were thought to be much higher than the national average. There were a large number of homeless families in the borough, one of the highest concentrations of 'rough sleepers' in Britain, and a highly visible population of alcohol and drug misusers.

Post-16 education provision in the borough was covered by seven comprehensive schools, two Further Education colleges, and many young people crossed borough boundaries both pre- and post-16. Work-based learning was restricted to the two colleges and only one private training provider, although there was a range of other providers in adjacent boroughs within reasonable travelling distance. However, less than a quarter of those following work-based routes entered Modern Apprenticeships, which was around half the proportion doing so nationally.

The size of the NEET group varied throughout 2003 from about 7.5% of the cohort in the autumn to 13.5% in the spring, although overall Metborough had the smallest number of NEET young people across the Partnership areas. Slightly more young men than women were defined as NEET with a third of the group coming from minority ethnic backgrounds.

Metro Connexions

Metro Connexions Partnership commenced operations in the summer of 2002. Under some opposition from the CSNU, Metro Connexions had stood out and was operating as a lead body Partnership. Given the diversity of the boroughs involved, reaching agreement to bid to be a lead body Connexions Partnership was a major achievement. The lead body arrangement meant that the legal ownership of the Partnership and contracting and financial services were provided by one of the local authorities covered by the Partnership. Like the other models, Metro Connexions had a Partnership Board and a LMC covering each of the local authorities. However, it was the lead body that supported the small central management team through service-level agreements with its key departments. Apart from these service-level agreements, Metro Connexions contracted for front-line services with a number of different providers. In this sense it was a variant of the subcontracting model rather than a direct delivery or transmuted model of Partnership delivery. The main contract holders included careers companies delivering mainstream careers education and guidance services to schools and colleges, as they were doing prior to the arrival of Connexions, together with the constituent local authorities.

Across Metborough there were 36 PAs employed by a number of contract holders. Fourteen PAs were employed by a careers company to carry out work in Metborough, although the company also served other local authorities. A further 22 were employed by the local authority Youth Service. According to estimates of the size of the cohort, this gave a higher PA to young person ratio than in either of the other two areas covered by the research. In Metborough the ratio averaged around 1:300, compared with 1:455 in Midland Connexions and 1:550 in Nortown. In principle this allowed PAs in Metborough much more time to spend on individual case studies and in developing interagency networks.

Initially, PAs employed by the Youth Service were managed by the Area Connexions Manager, who in turn was line-managed by the Head of Youth Services. During the course of the research, and following a consultant's report, these PAs became reorganised into three discrete teams, each with a manager responsible for the day-to-day supervision and support of the team. One of the teams offered extra support to schools, another supported the One-Stop-Shops and the third was a group of six PAs operating in a number of specialist settings: City of Metborough College, the Housing Assessment and Advice Centre, Medical Centre Children with Disabilities Team, the YOT, a Language Support Unit, and the Leaving Care Team in the social services department.

Issues in the development of partnership working in Metro Connexions and Metborough

Metro Connexions was one of the largest Partnerships in the country and covered the largest number of local authority areas in our study. It evolved from a series of pilot schemes in each of the boroughs. The chief executive (appointed in the summer of 2002) was a local manager of one of the pilots in 2001-02. He was therefore very knowledgeable about the areas in which the Partnership operated. Achieving partnership and an amicable consensus across all the boroughs was a remarkable achievement. The boroughs differed greatly in the problems they faced, their political complexion and their reputations for public services. At the time of the research Metborough was regarded as having a good record in education and social services.

The lead body model was the least widespread of the three models described in Chapter 1. Advantages included being able to draw on current expertise and systems such as financial systems and controls and procedures. There were clear advantages for the staff employed as PAs by the local authorities in terms of human resource structures, conditions of employment and pensions. Government Office and the CSNU were initially not convinced of the benefits and this opposition may have served to unite the authorities and careers companies in their determination. As a Board member explained, they knew that given initial opposition they would be subject to a:

> "much more detailed health check from the Government Office who did not like the idea of a lead body whatsoever and

would inspect us to death to prove that we'd got it wrong."

Many of those interviewed were strong supporters of the model, including some who had experience of working under different Partnerships adopting different models. As one of the key stakeholders argued:

> "If you take the [Metro Connexions] model, all of the legal services, you know, all of the corporate support services, personnel and the like, are provided on a contract. So the contract runs from the [Metro Connexions] Partnership [and] that contract with the [named] borough buys a service, it doesn't buy people ... you're buying a service contract, that's out-sourcing, and an extremely successful way of working...."

The same stakeholder also commented favourably on the way in which the Partnership had been developed with a strong voice from the different local authority areas:

> "...There's [also] a lot of subcontracted work which is managed by the boroughs, some of those people are then deployed in other places, OK, so they may ... be working on an outreach basis within one of the voluntary partners. But the thing that I like most about the way that the Metro Connexions model has gone is that plans have come up from the LMCs. It's much stronger from the ground upwards."

The location of those PAs not employed by the careers companies within the local authority Youth Service was seen by many of the stakeholders to have been a good idea and to have brought dividends in emphasising youth work, leisure and personal development as well as careers education and guidance. It had also enabled the development of a service drawing on a number of PAs with different specialist skills and expertise. A disadvantage was a potential split between the 'universal service' provided by careers PAs and the specialist and targeted service within the Youth Service. In the latter there were dangers of careers education and guidance (generic advice on post-16 education and training opportunities) being regarded as a taken-for-granted skill. Efforts were made during the course of the research to avoid this split in the service developing and to ensure proper referrals between the teams where appropriate. A protocol on referral and work sharing was being drawn up and joint meetings and away days were scheduled to take place.

Starting in 2004, Metro Connexions began a special project funded by the European Social Fund aimed at reducing the number of young people who were NEET. This enabled access to special funds of up to £1,000 per person on the project to help overcome barriers to work or training. There are similarities between this and the participation trial operating in Northern.

Northern and Nortown

Northern Connexions Partnership was large, complex, and covered around 180,000 young people aged 13-19 drawn from a number of different local authorities. It was served by four separate careers companies. Nortown was considered by the Chief Executive Officer of Northern Connexions as one of the biggest challenges. It had around 50,000 teenagers, spread across a large city, a number of small towns and a large rural area – three quarters of the district was classified as rural. Overall the district did not have a good record of educational achievement and also had clusters of young people from minority ethnic groups, constituting around one third of the school population. The analysis of need covered in the Connexions business plan did not indicate any over-representation of young people with SEN, or looked-after children in Nortown. However, the number of live births to women under the age of 20 and detected young offenders was a significantly higher proportion of the cohort than elsewhere in the subregion.

It was in the urban wards in Nortown where concentrations of non-white (mainly Pakistani) minority ethnic groups were to be found. The LLSC published an area-wide inspection of all 16-19 education and training provision in November 2002. This drew attention to different ethnic concentrations in adjacent schools. In one town within the district, for instance, 83% of its pupils came from minority ethnic groups whereas in another school (a religious foundation school) only 12% came from minority ethnic groups.

Promoting social cohesion was one of the four strategic aims and objectives of the LLSC five-year plan. While this social cohesion agenda was strongly represented in the LLSC planning, it did not appear to figure strongly in Connexions business planning. There appeared to be very little representation of the ethnic communities on the Connexions LMC in Nortown.

The LEA for Nortown had been regarded as a 'failing' authority in two recent OfSTED inspections and the education service was now run by a private company. Nortown had one of the lowest educational achievement rates in the subregion, although the Careers Destinations Survey for 2002-03 suggested some improvement. Pupils in Year 11 had low levels of achievement compared with the subregional and national averages. Just under 80% of 16-year-olds progressed into full-time education or training, although a comparatively low percentage proceeded to Further Education colleges. A careers destination survey indicated that approximately 14.5% of 16- to 18-year-olds were categorised as NEET in 2003 (a drop of 3.3% on the previous year). Minority ethnic groups were the least likely to find employment or higher levels of government-sponsored training but were much more likely than their white counterparts to be in general foundation training courses where they represented two thirds of all those placed in that sector.

Connexions in Northern

Connexions Northern was a subcontracting model of Partnership, and was a not-for-profit company limited by guarantee. The chief executive started in post in the spring of 2002 and the Partnership started operating in the autumn. A Partnership Board was responsible for the development of the Connexions Strategy across the subregion. The Board had 13 directors (and 22 members overall) and was composed of two directors from the careers companies, two from the local authorities, two from the voluntary sector, a head teacher, a representative from the strategic health authority, the police, and two directors from commercial organisations. It had an independent chair and vice-chair who, together with the chief executive, constituted the directors of the company. Members who attended the Board meetings as observers included the chairs of the LMCs. The Partnership

Board was supported by an Executive Management Team with around 30 staff, which was resourced by a 10% top-slice of the budget retained for central services and the strategic partnership.

The Partnership was seeking to promote multiagency work across the subregion through the issuing of multiple contracts to a variety of different service suppliers in the different local authorities. In each LMC area the major contract holders included a careers company, the LEA, the Youth Service and voluntary sector bodies. Some contracts were issued for the development of services across the subregion including, for instance, one to a voluntary sector organisation for support to young people in rural areas using mobile facilities.

The Board also supported a national initiative funded by the national Learning and Skills Council – a one-year 'participation trial'. This programme focused on support for four distinct groups of young people: those earning but not in learning; those at risk of dropping out from post-16 learning; those pre-16 at risk of not continuing in learning; and the 'hard-to-reach' NEET group. The 'trial' came with eight million pounds of extra resources to the subregion. This allowed for the employment of front-line workers who were called Key Workers (as distinct from Personal Advisers). As well as working with a small and targeted caseload, Key Workers could also access funds to help, support and reward young people's participation, and where necessary their learning or training costs. The funds could be used to support transport costs, or small items such as clothing or equipment that might make the difference between sustaining learning and dropping out. The Key Workers were employed directly by Connexions Northern and were located in a number of host agencies spread across the LMC areas. Nortown had a total of 11 Key Workers between April 2003 and March 2004 and reduced to four thereafter.

Connexions in Nortown

Each local authority had a Connexions Partnership Manager who was responsible for contract development (under the direction of the Partnership Board and the Chief Executive Officer) rather than managing the PAs employed by contract holders. In Nortown, the manager was also the key link between the subregional Board and the LMC. In line with similar developments across the subregion, the Manager also chaired an Implementation Group made up of the main Connexions contract holders in the district.

The major contract in the city of Nortown was with Careers Nortown, a private careers company. A 'core contract' funded a total of 61 full-time equivalent PAs at a cost of just under £3 million per year. Most of these PAs were working with young people in mainstream education and were school-based, although they also managed a Connexions Centre in Nortown. Only careers company PAs seemed to be based there and long-standing plans to locate others (including Jobcentre Plus benefits staff) did not come to fruition over the course of the research. Careers Nortown PAs included a Community Team composed of seven PAs from a variety of disciplinary backgrounds who previously worked with Learning Gateway clients. Now rebadged as Connexions PAs, they were working with young people at levels two or three of need (see Chapter 1). Half of the Nortown case studies (see Chapters 2 and 3) were drawn from this team. There was also a 'virtual team' working with young people with SEN, although mainly with those in special schools.

As well as these two teams, Careers Nortown also managed one PA seconded to the Independent Living Team, located in the social services department, who was working with care leavers and young people who were homeless. Another PA was seconded to the local YOT. However, these latter contracts were not issued until August 2003 so working practices and caseloads were not well-established. Careers Nortown had two additional PA posts, one to improve the involvement of young people, and another to help coordinate PAs across the area and promote a good practice forum.

The various Connexions contracts issued for Nortown covered the provision of just over 90 full-time equivalent PAs. Given the total number of 13- to 19-year-olds, if spread across the PAs equally, this would give a caseload of approximately 550 each. Some PAs, however, worked either with 'hard-to-reach' groups (those in danger of disengaging from education, employment and training) or with those who required intensive, and sometimes multi- or interagency, support. These PAs and the Key Workers were more likely to have a caseload of between 20-35, leaving those dealing with young people in mainstream education with caseloads of around nine hundred.

The appointment of specialist PAs other than the Careers Nortown Community Team was delayed due to difficulties in identifying and agreeing on their deployment and contracts. However, by the end of the fieldwork period, Further Education colleges had a contract to recruit a total of 4.5 full-time equivalent PAs, and the privatised LEA had a contract for nine PAs to work with school federations (issued in March 2004). Since November 2003, Nortown Youth Service and various specific organisations within the voluntary youth sector (since early in 2004) had contracts for a total of 14 PAs to carry out community-based work with the NEET group, although most were not in post until the spring. The full complement of PAs was, therefore, not in post until 18 months after the start date of Northern Connexions.

Issues in the development of partnership working in Northern and Nortown

From the outset there was a reluctance to accept the need for Connexions to be organised on a subregional basis. The cities (including Nortown) had hoped they were big enough to organise themselves (as they had done with YOTs and Drug Action Teams and other Partnerships) and sought to minimise the subregional influence of Connexions. The smaller boroughs were more positive about being part of a large subregion and saw dangers in being linked with only one big city. But they also saw few positive benefits of subregionality and many disadvantages. All those involved in the initial planning of Connexions in the subregion had hoped that the subcontracting partnership would allow for very significant delegation of authority and control to LMCs. The newly appointed chief executive, however, did not see his role or that of the Board as simply ratifying delegated decisions and passing on the resources:

> "As I said at my interview, so I was quite clear. I said, 'Do you want somebody to manage the subcontracting process and be a conduit for the money. If you want that – employ a pipe, all right!'. If you

want somebody to drive forward the Strategy and as part of that process operate a subcontracting model, then that's what I'm here to do...."

The first two years of the Partnership at Board level had been a site for conflict and acrimony, a reminder that forced collaboration between agencies can occasion antagonism, bitterness and dysfunctionality as well as cooperation, harmony and partnership. A number of different areas of grievance emerged. Those representing local authorities grumbled about the lack of consultation on the content of the second business plan, poor coordination of efforts in the contracting and deployment of the outreach facility, the direct employment of Key Workers under the participation trial, the need for a subregional computer system, and the long delays in the development of contracts to cover the full complement of PA posts across the districts. One of the avoidable sources of irritation and conflict concerned outreach work. News of the allocation of a Connexions contract for this 'leaked out' through an informal contact between youth work staff across the region with the vehicle supplier. When outreach finally started operating in Nortown, it did so in ways and at locations in which other interested parties thought to be singularly inappropriate and poorly targeted, and about which they had not been consulted. This caused some distrust and exasperation and was one of several instances where there was posturing and muscle-flexing between the subregion and the various members of Nortown LMC. The issue appeared to be resolved amicably when the interested parties finally met.

There were many accounts given to the researchers of how these and more fundamental issues had soured relationships between some of the major players. Frequently those within the careers companies, although supportive of the Connexions Strategy, saw it as a means of undermining the value of their activities. For instance, one said:

> "[Connexions] is a super concept and idea.... It's right [pause] but in implementation a great idea is being botched, and it's being botched for a number of reasons. One of which is I perceive that somebody somewhere has

decided they wanted to have a go at some of these careers companies."

All the careers company representatives interviewed initially saw Connexions as an opportunity for them to build on past experiences working with vulnerable groups but found that contract negotiations meant they were restricted to their previous responsibilities. As an example of some of the consequences of these conflicts, another Board member, not involved in any of these major battle fronts, told us:

> "It's felt frustrating, it's felt irritating, I've felt as if people were defending their own power and influence and not interested in ... looking at how the service was delivered to young people. I've felt that people were using ... their position on the Board of Northern not in any way for the best interests of Northern-led Connexions, but simply to defend their local authority. I've felt as if I was attending a 1958 meeting of the TUC.... In some senses I felt there was a determination to actually undermine what Connexions, Connexions Northern and that, you know, there was, the strategy was to make absolutely sure that it didn't work, if I'm totally honest with you...."

> "I have the choice of resigning from the Board of Connexions Northern, and I have seriously considered it ..., not because I can't deliver the loyalty, I can. It's because I am not sure I want to be part of such a, a vindictive and unpleasant battle of ... wills."

Some members of the Board clearly saw themselves as delegates of 'power blocks' (local authorities or careers companies) and networked accordingly. Other members 'representing' important spheres of activity (schools, youth justice and health, for instance) had no means of communicating with their 'constituency' and did not make any attempt to do so. They saw their Board membership as a means of bringing a 'perspective' or 'skills' to the Board rather than representing and/or communicating with interest groups.

One consequence of this was that the involvement of spheres of interest in Connexions

developments at a local authority level in Nortown was a little 'hit and miss'. For instance, the LMC had been unable to secure representation from schools and there remained considerable misunderstanding within schools about Connexions. Nortown YOT, the police, the Youth Service and the voluntary sector had active representation on the LMC but there was no direct representation from the Drug Action Team or Teenage Pregnancy Strategy. A wider group across the local authority covering health, education, social services, leisure, children's services had all cooperated in the development of a Children and Young People Strategic Plan (CYPSP), the coordinator for which was also a member of the LMC.

Many of those interviewed hoped that the conflict which was a feature of the first two years of the Partnership Board had come to a close. But it is worth noting that, as the fieldwork for the research was concluding, a further development in the relationships between the Partnership Board and the LMCs took place. As reported in Chapter 1, in January 2004 all Connexions Partnerships were told they were no longer eligible for VAT exemptions and would have to find the money from other sources. This provided yet another issue around which acrimonious disputes within the Partnership could reoccur. Bitterness and conflict between Board members, it seemed, persisted.

Also available from The Policy Press

Published in association with the Joseph Rowntree Foundation

Missing ConneXions

The career dynamics and welfare needs of black and minority ethnic young people at the margins

Liz Britton, Bob Coles, Gary Craig, Carl Hylton, Saira Mumtaz, Paul Bivand, Roger Burrows and Paul Convery

"... one of the most thorough, hard-hitting and important pieces of research findings that I have seen ... A must read." *Connexions Newscheck*

"... a useful addition to the literature on the subject of ethnicity, youth and exclusion." *Work, Employment and Society*

This report provides an account of a major evaluation of how existing services reach - or overlook - groups of the most disaffected young people. This is the first study focusing in particular on the needs and life experiences of young people from minority ethnic groups and the processes of exclusion which they experience.

Paperback £13.95 US$25.00 ISBN 1 86134 382 5
297 x 210mm 72 pages February 2002

Poor transitions

Social exclusion and young adults

Colin Webster, Donald Simpson, Robert MacDonald, Andrea Abbas, Mark Cieslik, Tracy Shildrick and Mark Simpson

This is a study of the longer-term transitions of young people living in neighbourhoods beset by the worst problems of social exclusion. Based on a rare example of longitudinal, qualitative research with 'hard-to-reach' young adults, the study throws into question common approaches to understanding and tackling social exclusion.

Paperback £13.95 US$23.95 ISBN 1 86134 650 6
297 x 210mm 56 pages December 2004

Snakes & Ladders

Young people, transitions and social exclusion

Les Johnston, Robert MacDonald, Paul Mason, Louise Ridley and Colin Webster

Existing research on young people has tended to ignore the different ways in which young people get by, grow up and make transitions to adulthood in areas labelled as socially excluded. This innovative report explores how young people from one particularly deprived area, facing the same limited opportunities and with similar socioeconomic backgrounds, follow diverse paths and reach strikingly different destinations in their early adulthood.

Paperback £11.95 US$19.95 ISBN 1 86134 290 X
297 x 210mm 44 pages October 2000

Losing out?
Socioeconomic disadvantage and experience in further and higher education
Alasdair Forsyth and Andy Furlong

Despite the recent expansion of higher education, representation, level of participation and likelihood of academic success remain highest amongst young people from affluent areas and lowest amongst those from deprived neighbourhoods. This report identifies the factors which impact upon the experiences of the minority of disadvantaged young people who enter higher education.

Paperback £14.95 US$25.50 ISBN 1 86134 508 9
297 x 210mm 76 pages May 2003

Socioeconomic disadvantage and access to higher education
Alasdair Forsyth and Andy Furlong

The gap in representation in higher education between affluent and disadvantaged young people continues. Through a survey of school-leavers, carried out both before and after leaving school, this detailed report explores the wide range of factors that affect young people's progress in this area. It concludes with policy recommendations for increasing disadvantaged young people's participation in higher education, making it vital reading for everyone interested in education and youth transitions.

Paperback £13.95 US$23.50 ISBN 1 86134 296 9
297 x 210mm 64 pages November 2000

Keeping track
Mapping and tracking vulnerable young people
Anne E. Green, Malcolm Maguire and Angela Canny

"Will be of particular assistance in business planning for Connexions and many others in guidence work ... excellent ... interesting, if not comfortable reading." *Connexions Newscheck*

Of particular concern to policy makers and practitioners involved in addressing social exclusion are the fortunes of vulnerable young people, especially those who have become detached from mainstream youth transitions. This useful report outlines some of the advantages and limitations of 'mapping' and 'tracking' methodologies. It identifies examples of good practice and difficulties which agencies have encountered in building reliable, accurate, up-to-date and robust systems.

Paperback £13.95 US$23.50 ISBN 1 86134 324
297 x 210mm 64 pages April 2001

To order further copies of this publication or any other Policy Press titles please contact:

In the UK and Europe:
Marston Book Services, PO Box 269, Abingdon,
Oxon, OX14 4YN, UK
Tel: +44 (0)1235 465500
Fax: +44 (0)1235 465556
Email: direct.orders@marston.co.uk

In the USA and Canada:
ISBS, 920 NE 58th Street, Suite 300, Portland, OR
97213-3786, USA
Tel: +1 800 944 6190 (toll free)
Fax: +1 503 280 8832
Email: info@isbs.com

In Australia and New Zealand:
DA Information Services, 648 Whitehorse Road
Mitcham, Victoria 3132, Australia
Tel: +61 (3) 9210 7777
Fax: +61 (3) 9210 7788
E-mail: service@dadirect.com.au

Further information about all of our titles can be
found on our website:

www.policypress.org.uk

211739

211739